LONG-TERM CARE
SUITABILITY

DEARBORN™
A **Kaplan Professional** Company

This publication is designed to provide accurate and authoritative information in regard to the subject matter covered. It is sold with the understanding that the publisher is not engaged in rendering legal, accounting or other professional service. If legal advice or other expert assistance is required, the services of a competent professional person should be sought.

This text is updated periodically to reflect changes in laws and regulations. To verify that you have the most recent update, you may call DEARBORN at 1-800-423-4723.

©2000 by Dearborn Financial Publishing, Inc.®
Published by Dearborn Financial Institute, Inc.®

Printed in the United States of America.

First printing, April 2000

Library of Congress Cataloging-in-Publication Data

Long-term care suitability.
    p. cm.
    ISBN 0–7931–3796-9
     1. Insurance, Long-term care—United States. 2. Insurance, Health—United
States. 3. Health Insurance Agents--United States. I. Dearborn Financial Institute.
  HG9390 .L66 2000
  368.38'2--dc21   00–028250

······ Table of Contents

······ Introduction

L ong-term care insurance is a relatively new insurance product. After a humble beginning, it gained a wider acceptance in the 1990s. There have been more than 5.8 million LTC policies sold through June of 1998. According to the Health Insurance Association of America, the sale of LTC policies increased by more than 580,000 in 1997 alone and by more than 300,000 policies during the first half of 1998. From 1987 to 1997, the annual rate of growth has averaged about 12 percent. More agents are selling the product and more companies are offering it than ever before. It is positioned to have exponential growth in the near future—but the growth won't come easy.

As the interest in long-term care insurance increases, questions arise and people seek answers. Agents try to learn enough about the product to sell it successfully. Insurance companies seek to understand enough to develop, price, administer and distribute it effectively. Consumers try to figure out what to look for in a policy and how much to pay for it. And regulators try to maintain a viable marketplace in which the product can be bought and sold.

Long-term care insurance provides no easy answers. What all interested parties must do is better understand the questions to ask. All have an interest in making long-term care insurance a valuable component of an individual's retirement planning. Accomplishing this will take time—time to work with one another, asking questions and listening to answers. This is especially important when an answer is not what we want or expect to hear.

Long-Term Care Suitability is a course designed to help insurance agents work with consumers. It will train agents in the process of educating prospects about the long-term care field and the need for long-term care insurance. The course will assist agents in the process of working with clients to design affordable policies tailored to meet their needs and goals. Agents who complete the course successfully will be able to:

- identify, understand and work effectively with prospects for long-term care insurance;

- help prospects understand what they need to know about the field of long-term care, particularly the health care professionals and organizations that provide long-term care services;

- educate prospects about the complexities of long-term care policies; and

- guide and advise prospects as they proceed step by step through the many decisions they must make in designing long-term care policies that meet their needs.

For practicality and to facilitate training, the course follows the traditional insurance sales process in teaching its lessons. It emphasizes suitability, the matching of product features and benefits to a prospect's needs and goals. The final chapter on case studies exemplifies the lessons of the course.

In the spirit of the traditional insurance sales process, the consumer is described in different ways throughout the text:

- as individuals, who have an unknown interest in long-term care insurance;

- as prospects, who meet with agents to discuss long-term care insurance;

- as applicants, who entrust agents to apply for long-term care insurance for them;

- as clients, who are approved for the insurance and accept the policies; and

- as claimants, who eventually qualify for benefits.

Most individuals ask the same questions:

- "Will I ever need care?"

- "How much will it cost then?"

- "How will I pay for it?"

Although the long-term care insurance dilemma provides no easy answers, time has a way of creating them. If agents wait too long to ask people questions about long-term care insurance, however, it may be too late for them to purchase the coverage.

This text provides the process to follow and the questions to ask to make suitable sales of LTC insurance policies. After finishing the text, an agent will know how to work with prospects to make them long-term care insurance clients. The key is to apply the knowledge quickly and frequently. Otherwise, time will provide other answers to people's questions—and they may be answers we don't want to hear, answers that don't meet clients' long-term care needs.

1

Suitability and Long-Term Care Insurance

W hat makes a long-term care (LTC) policy suitable? Some people believe suitability is determined by assessing a prospect's financial status. For these people, a sale is suitable when a prospect has a certain amount of assets and income. For example, the prospect may have to have retirement funds and an estate to protect. At a minimum, the prospect must be able to afford the policy.

Other people equate suitability with education. A sale is suitable when a prospect understands how an LTC policy works and why he or she is purchasing it. Market conduct investigations that resulted in multimillion dollar fines against insurance companies have focused attention on this aspect of the LTC insurance policy sales process.

To still others, the essential component of a suitable sale is the identification of a prospect's needs and the matching of appropriate policy features and benefit levels to those needs. To these people, the measure of a suitable sale is when a claim is filed and the insured receives the type and level of benefits needed.

An LTC insurance policy is a complex and evolving product that is difficult to understand, design and manage. Furthermore, it's a new product to consumers, agents, insurers and insurance regulators. This chapter explores the meaning of suitability and the related concerns of each of these players. These concerns arise from the questions, uncertainties and confusion surrounding a relatively new and rapidly evolving product.

■ ■ ■ ■ ■

■ CONCERNS OF CONSUMERS

An LTC insurance policy is so new to most consumers that they have no personal experience to guide them in investigating and purchasing the product. Their parents didn't own LTC insurance, and few, if any, of their friends have LTC policies. Practically no one knows anyone who actually received benefits from an LTC policy. On the other hand, many people know someone who needed LTC and had to pay for it out of his or her own pocket with dire consequences.

The decision to buy LTC insurance is difficult to make because LTC is a new, evolving and complex product that prospects must understand to make the many decisions involved in designing policies that meet their needs. The process is made more difficult for prospects because they have no experience to guide them in choosing the right policies. Articles in popular magazines are inconclusive about whether LTC insurance is a need, as the insurance industry claims, or a waste of time and money. Too often, these articles give confusing mixed messages. The National Association of Insurance Commissioners (NAIC) has published *A Shopper's Guide to Long-Term Care Insurance*, which provides helpful tips. The guide must be given to consumers for disclosure purposes in many states. Remarkably, this guide also is unconvincing when it comes to deciding whether LTC insurance is a wise investment.

Few companies educate consumers about why they should consider purchasing LTC insurance, and fewer still guide them in choosing suitable policies. Too often, companies that do try to educate consumers mix their educational materials with sales literature, a practice that causes confusion and is unappreciated by consumers.

Some of the best information about LTC insurance is on the Internet; however, this information presents all sorts of credibility issues to consumers—especially seniors, who tend to be leery of information in cyberspace. Is the information factual? Is it honest and objective? Also, while many prospects for LTC insurance are computer savvy and access the Internet regularly, they are not ready yet to buy insurance on the web.

Consumer advocates advise each prospect to speak to many agents before deciding to buy a particular LTC policy. Of course, this results in confusion and uncertainty about whether the prospect will buy from the right agent and the right company. Other than using a financial rating, few LTC insurance prospects know how to evaluate an insurance company. The purchase of an LTC policy requires a prospect to search his or her innermost feelings about a subject that is difficult to consider in private, let alone in front of a stranger. Consumers don't want to go through that experience repeatedly with various agents they hardly know.

So what should a consumer do? Go through the experience repeatedly with various agents or purchase a policy from the first agent the prospect trusts? Faced with this choice, many consumers simply procrastinate. They delay the purchase decision, which may be the worst decision for a consumer.

■ CONCERNS OF LIFE INSURANCE AGENTS AND FINANCIAL PLANNERS

Because LTC insurance is so new and evolving so rapidly, life insurance agents and financial planners face many of the same issues consumers face. They voice concerns about whether their clients need LTC insurance policies, which companies provide the best products, and how the agents and planners can identify quality products. Their clients ask them about the advisability of purchasing LTC insurance, and they don't know what advice to give.

Agents read the same magazine articles consumers read. They also read the NAIC's *A Shopper's Guide to Long-Term Care Insurance*. Because the primary insurers many agents have done business with for years do not offer long-term care insurance, the agents are forced to conduct their own analyses to identify which companies offer the best products for their clients. Wholesalers tout their wares to life insurance agents, promoting different LTC products. Some of these products cover only home care. Some are presented as riders to life insurance policies. Some cover only certain types of facilities, while others are comprehensive, covering everything.

It seems like everyone has advice to give, but—as mentioned earlier—LTC insurance provides no easy answers. Some say an insurer's financial strength and ratings are essential. Others recommend finding the policy with the best features. Some represent companies with cheap rates as all insurance companies try to establish their niches in this market, which provides untapped potential. Many attorneys favor the transfer of assets and reliance on Medicaid. Everyone seems to be jockeying for position. As a result, many agents are confused and fearful of not being able to offer the best advice to their prospects and clients.

Agents seek reliable and objective information that gives them the knowledge to sell LTC insurance with comfort and confidence. Unfortunately, they're not finding such information. Instead, they read trade journals that publish articles about companies that underprice their products to gain market share, with the intention of raising rates in the future. Such articles make agents believe all companies are engaged in similar practices, and they don't want their clients to be subjected to premium increases every year. Other articles fuel the debate that's raging about whether it's better to purchase a tax-qualified or a nontax-qualified LTC policy.

Agents also have questions about how to design an LTC plan. For example, why is inflation protection so expensive? Is it worth the price? How does the elimination period work? Should an agent recommend a tax-qualified or a nontax-qualified policy? What distinguishes a reimbursement plan from an indemnity plan? Because they don't know the answers to such questions, they don't talk about LTC insurance. They continue selling the products they've always sold. They have decided not to take the time to learn about a product surrounded by so much complexity and uncertainty. Meanwhile, a huge and lucrative opportunity awaits agents with the know-how to take advantage of the challenge LTC insurance presents.

Agents who take advantage of this opportunity find that they can use the LTC sales process to acquire a prospect's trust. Once that trust is established, it is easy to take the next step and evaluate the client's overall financial situation and the opportunities available for additional products and services.

■ CONCERNS OF INSURANCE COMPANIES

Several big issues face insurance companies. One is whether to offer an LTC product. Another involves defining the characteristics of an LTC product to offer. Still another concerns the appropriate pricing of an LTC product. All these issues must be resolved amidst considerable uncertainty.

The decision-makers at insurance companies read the same articles consumers and agents read. Everyone—consumers, agents, insurers—wants to know whether LTC insurance is a viable product. The evidence favoring such a product is building. A growing number of insurance companies realize that LTC insurance provides benefits their clients need. With increasing longevity, more and more of these clients

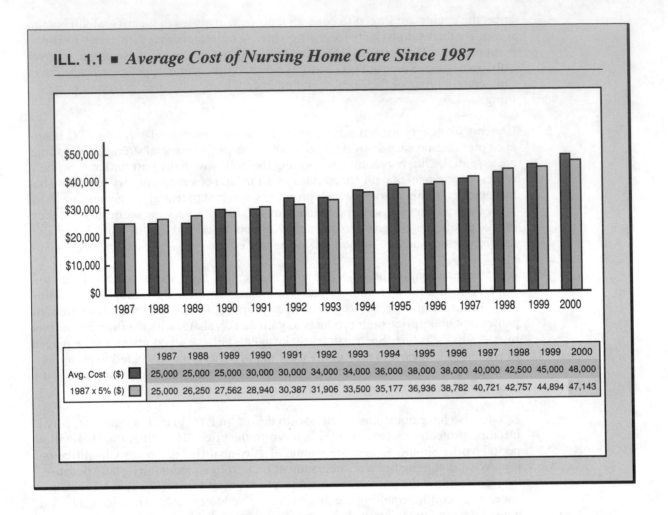

ILL. 1.1 ■ *Average Cost of Nursing Home Care Since 1987*

	1987	1988	1989	1990	1991	1992	1993	1994	1995	1996	1997	1998	1999	2000
Avg. Cost ($)	25,000	25,000	25,000	30,000	30,000	34,000	34,000	36,000	38,000	38,000	40,000	42,500	45,000	48,000
1987 x 5% ($)	25,000	26,250	27,562	28,940	30,387	31,906	33,500	35,177	36,936	38,782	40,721	42,757	44,894	47,143

are cashing in their life insurance policies and annuities to pay for LTC services, which isn't good for the insureds or the insurers. LTC insurance solves this problem.

Everyone is aware of the demographic shift described as the *graying of America*. In 1997, about 34 million people in the United States were age 65 or older, and this group is living longer than ever before. The older population will burgeon between the years 2010 and 2030, when the baby boomers (those born between 1946 and 1964) reach age 65. By 2030, about 70 million older persons will live in the United States, more than twice their number in 1997. People older than age 65 will represent 13 percent of the population in 2000 and 20 percent of the population in 2030. Add to this the fact that people older than age 85 make up the fastest growing segment of the entire population, and the odds of entering a nursing home and staying for an extended period increase with age. An average nursing home today costs about $48,000 a year, and the average length of stay is 2½ years. Given these numbers and trends, LTC insurance is a product that makes increasing sense to purchase.

Everyone has an opinion about what aging people want and need, and quite often these opinions don't jive with reality. For example, many insurers believe older

Americans need less life insurance, so they search for ways to diversify their product offerings. However, it's a known fact that most people are grossly underinsured for life insurance. Some companies think LTC insurance is an easy sale because so few people own it, but LTC insurance isn't suitable for all companies and all distribution systems.

Is it suitable to offer a product that has so many unknowns, so much uncertainty? Is long-term care an insurable event? Insurance covers dreaded events—like death, robberies and car crashes. Some people think the likelihood of a claim is so high that LTC insurance cannot be priced properly. Data used to price LTC policies are based on the costs of using services, not on how insureds act when they need LTC services. Few companies have enough experience to price their products based on their own data. For example, do seniors want strangers coming into their homes to help them when they are unable to care for themselves? Or would they prefer to move to facilities where others perform household chores and where health care and other services are available?

Introducing a new product like LTC insurance is a complicated process for an insurance company. First, the company must design and price the product carefully to meet the needs of its distribution system and to provide financial returns commensurate with the risk undertaken. Then the insurance company must struggle to gain approval of the product in various states. State-specific modifications must be made, and multiple disclosure forms and booklets must be prepared. Advertising materials must be submitted to state insurance departments, which invariably require modifications before the materials can be used. This isn't an easy procedure for companies, which must devote considerable resources to the process to succeed.

Finally, the company must ensure that its new product is sold in a suitable manner. Some companies and regulators make agents complete suitability worksheets (required in many states), but many people question whether this is an accurate measure of a true suitability assessment. Other companies test their agents' product knowledge and ability to identify the need for LTC insurance.

Having gone through this process, the insurance company learns that demographics don't buy policies, well-informed individuals do. Redesigning a distribution system and motivating the system's agents to sell a new and complex product is difficult. The company must provide extensive training using multiple media to help agents understand why and how to offer the new product in a suitable way. All in all, the company must devote considerable resources to introducing a new product in order to succeed in the process.

■ CONCERNS OF REGULATORS

Regulators try to balance the needs of both insurance companies and the public in drafting regulations and legislation and in approving each insurance company's policy forms, disclosure documents and advertising materials. Insurance regulators have been the most vocal in expressing their concerns about suitability. They have seen the product evolve from one that mirrored Medicare's requirements for benefits to today's policies that provide meaningful benefits.

In the middle 1980s, a company could offer a product that was conditionally renewable and require a three-day hospitalization to qualify for benefits. Just 15 years ago, some states imposed no long-term care regulations, and the regulations of those states that did were weak. Today, every state reviews products and forms, and many states have rate approval authority and review advertising filings. Companies must modify their contracts, disclosure documents and advertising materials to comply with regulations. Thankfully, the days of offering illusionary benefits in a cancelable contract are long gone.

Today's LTC policy typically covers skilled, intermediate and custodial care in state-licensed nursing homes, as well as home health services provided by state-licensed or Medicare-certified home health care agencies. Many policies also cover adult day care services and other care in the community. Companies today also must offer inflation protection, a nonforfeiture option, a third-party notification of lapse, a guaranteed renewable contract and other consumer-friendly features. The Health Insurance Portability and Accountability Act of 1996 (HIPAA) made consumer protection a large part of a tax-qualified plan's requirements. And on the horizon are more stringent regulations regarding rate stability.

Regulators have seen a few companies enter the LTC insurance industry and then leave it by selling their blocks of business. Eventually, the insureds whose policies were sold suffered rate hikes. Regulators don't want to see this happen too frequently. State insurance departments exist to minimize this type of activity.

Regulators strive to hold companies accountable for making suitable sales and fulfilling the promises made to insureds at the time of sale. Congress has investigated LTC insurance sales practices, and state market conduct exams and rating agency investigations have begun to include long-term care. The IMSA plans to include independent assessments of long-term care in the year 2001. Suitability and agent conduct frequently are part of the write-up of these evaluations. It is essential that agents remain aware of what they say and that they do not fudge the truth to make a sale.

Specifically, what makes an LTC insurance sale suitable? For example, is it suitable when:

- the consumer makes an informed decision and the policy meets the consumer's needs and budget, now and in the future?

- the agent provides the factual information and disclosures the consumer needs to make an informed decision?

- the company fulfills its promise to provide meaningful benefits and stable premiums while maintaining its ability to stay in business?

- regulators maintain a trustworthy marketplace and foster innovation?

A yes answer to each of these questions seems to satisfy all the players and create a perfect market. This brief overview of some of the major concerns of consumers, agents, insurance companies and regulators provides a sense of the uncertainties surrounding LTC insurance. Obviously, it's all very confusing.

■ SUITABILITY IN ACTION

Suitability is not a precise term in the insurance industry. Already in this text, it has been used to describe many areas of the sales cycle. Suitability is not a black or white issue. Many gray areas exist between being suitable and unsuitable.

Most agents understand that any product they recommend should be affordable and meet a prospect's needs. But suitability drives deeper than that. Today, given the newness of long-term care insurance and the uncertainties surrounding it, suitability also requires attention to the prospect's ability to understand and manage the recommended product. Suitability depends as much on the prospect's capabilities as his or her needs.

This adds to an agent's challenge. Agents need the skills not only to understand and present the product in layman's terms, but also to assess thoroughly a prospect's needs, wants and financial situation. Much of this is addressed in Chapter 4, "Fact Finding and Analysis." Agents also must educate clients so they can make informed decisions in designing and managing their LTC policies.

For this text, suitability focuses on the relationship between a recommended product and the client's needs and capabilities. For each prospect, on a case-by-case basis, suitability is determined by asking the following questions and analyzing the answers:

- What are the individual's needs and wants?

- What products can help meet those needs?

- Does the individual understand the product and its provisions?

- Is the individual capable of managing the product?

- Is the agent's recommendation in the prospect's best interests?

What are the individual's needs and wants?

In every LTC insurance sale, the principle of suitability demands an answer to the question, "What are the individual's needs?" LTC can meet various needs, such as to protect assets, provide options in care providers, maintain a person's independence so as not to burden children and avoid ever-changing government programs. Where a need or desire for financial protection exists, so does the potential for a suitable sale.

The fact finder in this text helps agents assess a prospect's needs and desires. It looks at both facts about the prospect and his or her feelings. Purchasing long-term care insurance is both a logical and an emotional decision. A suitable sale occurs when an applicant knows the policy is right for him or her, both logically and emotionally.

What products can help meet those needs?

Conceptually, long-term care insurance is a simple product. When someone loses his or her ability to remain independent, the person receives money to pay for care.

In actuality, it is much more complicated. Five basic choices must be made. Within those choices are many options. Different companies offer different options. Some companies offer benefit choices beyond the five basics.

Consequently, before a specific product is recommended, an agent must examine many other issues, including the:

- prospect's reason for purchasing the coverage;

- nature of the insurance need (temporary or long term);

- individual's ability to pay the premium for the extent of the need;

- prospect's sensitivity to price and the cost/benefit trade-off associated with that sensitivity;

- individual's willingness to reapply for and purchase additional coverage in the future;

- integration of LTC insurance with existing insurance coverage and the complete retirement plan;

- individual's need or desire for product flexibility;

- likelihood that the individual's needs will change in the foreseeable future; and

- individual's tolerance for risk versus his or her desire—or need—for guarantees.

Evaluating these factors places the agent in a far better position to make a suitable product recommendation. Doing so is the essence of needs analysis, which everyone agrees is the best way to determine the type and amount of insurance protection an individual should have. The quality of an agent's services and the suitability of his or her recommendations are related directly to the kind of analysis the agent offers.

Does the individual understand the product and its provisions?

It is not enough to determine a prospect's needs and recommend an appropriate solution. If the applicant does not understand the product or its provisions, a suitable sale has not been made.

Agents must educate prospects and fully explain a product's features and benefits. Given the newness of LTC insurance, this is essential. Prospects are exposed to jargon they never have heard before and frequently don't question unfamiliar terms because they are afraid of appearing ignorant or uninformed. Agents must recognize this challenge and spend extra time explaining contractual provisions to prospects.

Any preconceived notions a prospect has about a product must be explored, and any misconceptions must be dispelled before an agent takes an application. This requires skill in asking the right questions and listening to the answers, in terms of both the words and the level of confidence in the prospect's voice. The agent must know how the product functions, how it is expected to perform, the needs it fills and how it fits into the prospect's total financial or retirement plan. This all takes time and patience.

Is the individual capable of managing the product?

In trying to determine an individual's ability to manage an LTC insurance policy, an agent often focuses too much attention on the prospect's ability to pay premiums, now and in the future. Well-trained and qualified agents work with prospects in assessing their financial situations and determining whether excess income exists to pay the long-term care insurance premiums. Then the prospects are asked to get out their crystal balls, so to speak, and try to identify possible changes in their finances in the future. Will these changes affect the eventual affordability of premiums? This is just the first of many steps involved in assessing a prospect's capability of managing the product.

LTC insurance products present an element of uncertainty to buyers. The choices to be made differ from the choices involved in purchasing other insurance products. And the options within those choices are extensive. Furthermore, a client's circumstances can change quickly; for example, a spouse can die or an investment can fail. Retired people worry about having enough money to last their lifetimes because they know they can't go back to work at their last salaries to rebuild their retirement nest eggs. Circumstances change, and consequently, choices made yesterday are not the same choices a person might make today. All this can create considerable anxiety.

Clients should not have to manage their LTC insurance alone. A professional insurance agent maintains and nurtures permanent relationships with his or her clients. This alleviates much of the anxiety people feel about retirement and LTC. Over time, the agent may need to make adjustments under the following circumstances:

- If a policy does not include inflation protection, the agent may have to adjust the daily benefit as the cost of care increases.

- The agent may have to adjust the elimination period after a client receives an inheritance and is willing to pay more out of pocket for the cost of care.

- The agent may have to adjust the benefit maximum because a spouse dies and the widow's income is reduced significantly.

- The agent may have to adjust the covered providers because the only home care agency in an area goes out of business.

- The agent may have to adjust the inflation protection because the cost of care is rising at an unexpectedly high or low rate.

Is the agent's recommendation in the prospect's best interests?

An insurance agent has one principal reason for calling on a prospect: to offer a product that will benefit that person. The agent must determine what is beneficial in relation to the totality of the prospect's situation: his or her needs, understanding, knowledge, motivation, acceptance and means.

A long-term care policy offering $250 a day with automatic inflation and an unlimited maximum will benefit almost all individuals, but it is not practical or suitable for everyone. It is never in a prospect's best interests to buy more insurance than he or she can afford.

Suitability demands that the recommended product address the best interests of the prospect, not the producer. Putting the prospect's interests first ultimately serves the agent best. This fosters a relationship-driven, consultative approach to the agent's sales efforts and helps build the kind of client relationships that produce repeat business and referrals—the lifeblood of successful agents.

The rules of suitability are not precise, but at the same time they are not complex. The integrity of agents who follow one common sense rule will not be questioned: *Don't recommend an option that doesn't fit a prospect's needs or wants.* Therefore, an agent who manipulates a product recommendation to put his or her own needs (for a higher commission) before those of a client violates this simple rule. The agent who bases his or her recommendations on a client's needs, abilities and best interests conforms to the spirit of suitability.

Some people feel that a conflict of interest exists in having agents involved in such an important decision as LTC insurance. After all, most agents receive their compensation for making sales, not just for providing information or service. However, an agent will not make a sale unless the prospect is assured the agent is working in the prospect's best interests. Plus, most prospects need an agent to educate and motivate them to make a decision. An agent executing a suitable sale is an advocate for his or her client.

The pledge of the Chartered Life Underwriter (CLU) sums up the spirit of proper suitability:

> *In all my professional relationships, I pledge myself to the following rule of ethical conduct: I shall, in light of all conditions surrounding those I serve, which I shall make every effort to ascertain and understand, render that service which, in the same circumstances, I would apply to myself.*

■ SUMMARY

No single definition for suitability exists. It is one of those concepts, like character, that you know when you see it. Regulators, consumers, agents and insurers all strive to achieve a perfect balance among each other's needs to create the perfect market.

Suitability is achieved when a consumer makes the difficult decision to purchase an LTC insurance policy. Many entities and dedicated individuals have worked to shape the product into the viable insurance tool it is today, a product poised for widespread acceptance. This will happen only if agents, insurers and regulators strive to balance each others' interests in a spirit of cooperation for the purpose of making all sales of LTC insurance policies suitable.

■ CHAPTER 1 QUESTIONS FOR REVIEW

1. In the process of selling an LTC policy, which of the following must an agent give to the consumer for disclosure purposes?

   A. *A Shopper's Guide to Long-Term Care Insurance*
   B. Prospectus for the policy
   C. List of competitive products sold in the area
   D. List of the facilities and services in the area available to the insured when needed

2. All of the following terms describe an LTC insurance policy EXCEPT

   A. complex
   B. evolving
   C. new
   D. inexpensive

3. Which of the following is NOT a concern of consumers?

   A. No experience to guide them in purchasing LTC policies
   B. Determining whether the need for LTC is an insurable event
   C. Understanding a complex product
   D. Determining whether an LTC policy is a viable product

4. Which of the following is NOT a concern of insurance agents?

   A. How to design a quality LTC policy
   B. Determining whether an LTC policy is a viable product
   C. Redesigning a distribution system to sell LTC insurance
   D. Identity of an insurer that offers the best product for clients

5. Which of the following statements about suitability is NOT true?

   A. The higher the cost, the more suitable a product.
   B. A client can afford a suitable product.
   C. A client can manage a suitable product.
   D. A suitable product meets a client's logical and emotional needs.

2

Evolution of Long-Term Care Insurance

T he need for LTC insurance has grown dramatically in recent years as more and more people live into their 80s and 90s. In the past, most Americans died before their bodies began to wear down and developed chronic conditions. Also, the cost of care was not the national issue it is today. Many people could afford the $10,000 to $15,000 a year it cost for nursing home care. Finally, the budgets of the traditional outside payment sources, such as children or government programs like Medicaid, are stretched thin now. The high and always rising cost of care today has caused these outside sources to change the way they pay for care.

The average annual cost of nursing home care in the United States today, in the year 2000, is $48,000, a figure that increases about 5 percent each year. Receiving professional LTC services in the home can be even more expensive, particularly if the recipient needs care 24 hours a day. Because such costs can be devastating to a person's retirement nest egg, many agents and financial practitioners believe LTC insurance is a necessary component of any comprehensive financial plan. They also have an ethical, if not fiduciary, responsibility to present LTC insurance for their clients' consideration.

It hasn't always been this way. Older policies were not as reliable at claim time as today's policies. Through the years, however, regulators, consumer advocates and insurers with their consultants have molded the products to better meet the expectations and needs of claimants. Many professional insurance agents, having recognized these valuable changes, have integrated LTC insurance into their product lines.

This chapter explores the evolution of LTC insurance policies. Although LTC insurance is not a recent innovation, *quality* LTC insurance is relatively new. Understanding the history of the product will help agents better evaluate prospects' existing coverage and design suitable solutions to their current needs. It also will help agents understand why products are designed the way they are today.

■ ■ ■ ■ ■

■ ORIGINAL POLICIES

Long-term care insurance first appeared after Medicare was established in 1965. Although Medicare was designed to help older Americans pay for their health care expenses after they retired and no longer had the group medical insurance provided by their employers, it wasn't intended to cover all health care expenses for people older than 65. The government left gaps in Medicare's coverage, including copayments and deductibles, which people had to pay out of their own pockets. Consumers wanted additional insurance to cover these and other personal expenditures.

Insurance companies responded by offering Medicare-supplement insurance to cover Medicare's copayments and deductibles, as well as nursing home insurance to supplement Medicare's limited coverage for skilled nursing care. No experience or data served as a basis for developing LTC policy features and benefits or for setting premiums and predicting claims. As a result of this lack of experience, the original policies were modeled after Medicare requirements because Medicare was perceived as setting the standard for quality coverage. The goal was limited claims. Nursing home insurance has evolved significantly since that time. The products offered today are much more responsive to consumer needs than those offered just 15 years ago.

■ EVOLUTION OF BENEFIT CRITERIA

The initial nursing home insurance policies mirrored Medicare's requirements for payment of benefits. To qualify for benefits, an insured had to:

- spend three days in a hospital;

- enter a Medicare-certified skilled nursing facility; and

- receive skilled nursing care.

Skilled nursing care is daily, restorative care, ordered by a physician and delivered by skilled personnel. For Medicare's purposes, daily means five days a week; restorative care is rehabilitation treatment or therapy to assist an individual's continuing recovery; ordered by a physician means the primary doctor certifies that care is needed for the same condition for which a person received hospital treatment; and skilled personnel means qualified nurses—RNs or LPNs.

In the late 1970s and early 1980s, the delivery of health care began to change as a result of efforts to contain soaring Medicare costs. To stop health care costs from rising, the government implemented a series of measures that reversed the incentives in the Medicare system. Whereas the old system encouraged health care providers to render as many services as possible in order to cure their Medicare patients, the new system encourages them to provide the fewest services necessary. Furthermore, while the old system promoted the use of the most intensive and expensive care settings (hospitals), the new system encourages the use of less intensive and expensive care settings (LTC facilities, patient's homes).

Under the old Medicare system, physicians charged what were called *usual, customary and reasonable fees*. Medicare paid a physician's full fee if it did not exceed his or her usual charge; if it did not exceed the amount customarily charged for the

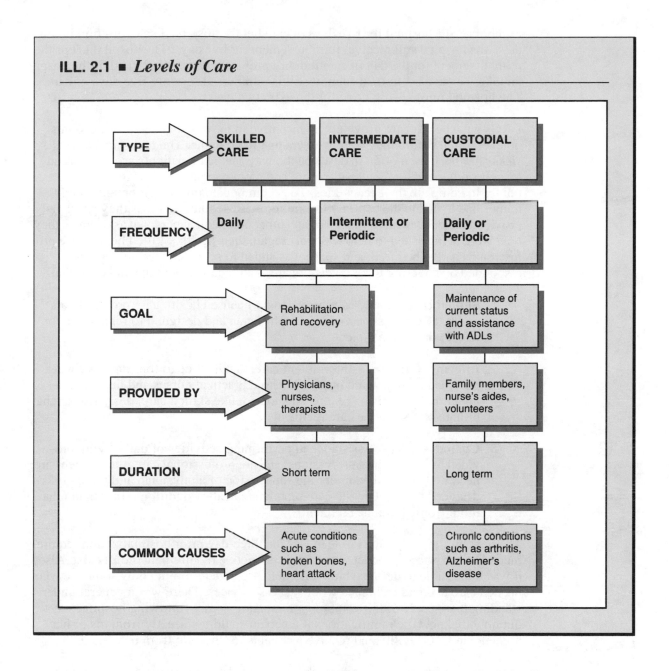

ILL. 2.1 ■ *Levels of Care*

service by other doctors in the area; or if it was justified by a given patient's specific circumstances. The new system, called the *Prospective Payment System*, sets the amount that Medicare will pay for services before the services are provided. The amount paid is based on the average cost of treating a particular condition, regardless of the number of services received or the length of a patient's stay in a hospital.

For example, if John is diagnosed as having a broken arm, he is admitted to the hospital under that diagnosis-related group (DRG). Medicare has established a prospective price for that broken arm, and that is the amount the hospital will receive from Medicare for treating John, no matter how long or short his stay and no matter what services the hospital performs to treat him. If the DRG for John's injury reimburses the hospital for five days of care but the hospital discharges him in four days, the hospital still receives reimbursement for five days. The hospital keeps the reimbursement for the day of care it didn't provide. On the other hand, if the hospital takes seven days to treat John, it still is reimbursed for only five days of care. The hospital must absorb costs for the extra two days.

DRGs gave health care providers an incentive to move patients out of hospitals quicker, often before they were well enough to go home. The term *quicker and sicker* has been used often to describe the way Medicare patients are discharged from hospitals today. As a result, more and more patients were sent to nursing homes to complete their recoveries. To accommodate this development, nursing homes had to create the capacity to care for these people. Whereas they previously provided residents with room, board and other nonmedical personal assistance, they now were being asked to help residents regain their health. Skilled health care professionals had to be hired, and space was added to provide therapies. Insurers responded by covering three levels of care—skilled, intermediate and custodial.

1. **Skilled care**—Daily care provided by licensed health care professionals under the direct supervision of a physician and designed to rehabilitate or restore the care recipient.

2. **Intermediate care**—Intermittent care, that is three to four days per week provided by registered nurses, licensed practical nurses and nurses' aides under the supervision of a physician and, like skilled care, designed to rehabilitate or restore the care recipient.

3. **Custodial care**—Assistance in performing activities of daily living provided by a number of professional and nonprofessional caregivers. Such care need not be provided under the supervision of a physician and typically is designed to maintain the care recipient's health condition rather than rehabilitate or restore the recipient.

The next hurdle for insurers to leap was the three-day prior hospitalization requirement. Data to price a product without this restrictive requirement didn't exist. Also, it was impossible to define which criteria to use in determining how someone who needed care and had insurance would access services. There was a general understanding that people didn't want to go to nursing homes following hospital stays, but nobody knew the ramifications if a person could go directly from his or her home to an LTC facility and receive payments for the care from insurance.

Some insurers developed products that required claimants to need medically necessary care without any prior hospitalization. Some companies tried to define *medically necessary*, but most left the term vague and undefined. The most important development, however, occurred when all the requirements Medicare imposes on its beneficiaries were eliminated. In other words, long-term care insurance no longer was tied to any of Medicare's criteria. The result was a product consumers and insurance professionals began to accept.

Nursing home insurance had separated itself successfully from Medicare by the time Medicare's requirements were scrutinized by Congress next. In the landmark Medicare Catastrophic Health Care Act of 1988, Medicare's three-day prior hospitalization requirement was lifted, and the skilled nursing benefits could last up to

---

ILL. 2.2 ■ *Activities of Daily Living (ADLs)*

Bathing	The ability to wash oneself by spongebath; or in either a tub or shower, including the tasks of getting into or out of the tub or shower.
Dressing	The ability to put on and take off all items of clothing and any necessary braces, fasteners or artificial limbs.
Toileting	The ability to get to and from the toilet, get on and off the toilet, and perform associated personal hygiene.
Transferring	The ability to move in and out of a bed, chair or wheelchair.
Continence	The ability to maintain control of bowel and bladder function or, when unable to maintain control of bowel or bladder function, the ability to perform associated personal hygiene (including caring for catheter or colostomy bag).
Eating	The ability to feed oneself by getting food into the body from a receptacle (such as a plate, cup or table), or by a feeding tube, or intravenously.

---

150 days. Many thought this was the beginning of the end for the private nursing home insurance industry.

Instead, companies and agents who understood Medicare's requirements found that this expansion made the limitations of Medicare more obvious. State-of-the-art LTC insurance plans covered all levels of care in any type of nursing home, while Medicare still required skilled care to be delivered in a Medicare-certified skilled nursing facility. Because of Medicare's limited expansion, more and more people learned about the incomplete coverage the government made available. Furthermore, the 1988 act was repealed in 1989.

The medical necessity trigger continued to gain acceptance from consumers and agents; however, insurers wanted objective criteria to guide them in paying benefits only when appropriate. To formulate these criteria, they turned to their consultants for advice, and in 1988, the first benefit guidelines based on physical and cognitive measures were introduced.

Clinical researchers began looking for ways to measure an individual's need for care in the 1960s. Sidney Katz recognized that healthy people took for granted certain common tasks, while impaired people needed assistance with them. These tasks are called *activities of daily living (ADLs)*.

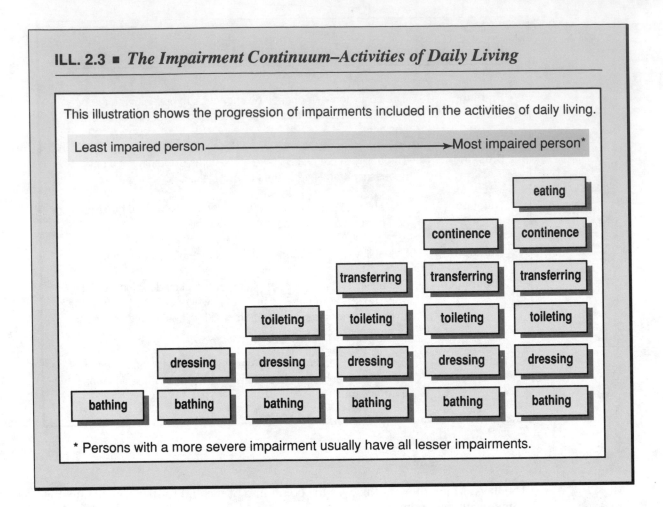

ILL. 2.3 ■ *The Impairment Continuum–Activities of Daily Living*

This illustration shows the progression of impairments included in the activities of daily living.

Least impaired person————————————————→Most impaired person*

eating

continence | continence

transferring | transferring | transferring

toileting | toileting | toileting | toileting

dressing | dressing | dressing | dressing | dressing

bathing | bathing | bathing | bathing | bathing | bathing

* Persons with a more severe impairment usually have all lesser impairments.

One of the problems insurers had to solve to use ADLs as benefit criteria was how to assess claimants' ability to accomplish them. Insurers didn't want their claim representatives flying all over the country to perform assessments. The problem was solved when trained independent assessors emerged throughout the country. These assessors are educated in geriatrics and are either registered nurses or social workers with master's degrees. Their arms-length assessments provide the objectivity insurers need.

Another problem insurers tackled in using ADLs as benefit criteria involved trying to determine whether claimants were simply unwilling or really unable to perform ADLs. To solve the dilemma, researchers developed a series of questions that assessors use as part of their analyses.

Researchers also found that some people needed assistance in remembering when and how to perform ADLs. These *cognitive impairments* are harder to measure than ADL impairments because the determination involves evaluating intelligence versus ability to think or perceive. Today, multiple measures are used to determine accurately a person's ability to reason, remember and remain oriented.

Companies have found these tools so reliable in assessing claimants' needs for benefits that they now can use the measures for underwriting. In fact, some assessments are conducted over the phone rather than in person. In either case, the assessments form the basis of a tax-qualified plan's qualification criteria.

■ EXPANDING PROVIDERS OF CARE

During the product evolution boom of the 1980s, the traditional providers of care expanded. Moving away from Medicare's requirements, private nursing home insurance was, at last, able to take advantage of the latest data on nursing home use. LTC policies began to pay for benefits in settings other than Medicare-certified skilled nursing facilities. For example, insurance companies designed policies that paid for care in nursing homes licensed as custodial care facilities and in skilled care facilities that weren't Medicare certified.

Consumers applauded this liberalization of benefits and asked for more. For instance, Medicare's home care benefit covered 21 days of care. Couldn't insurers offer more? At the time, home care was a new and emerging health care industry.

Insurers felt entering a nursing home was an insurable event, but they hesitated to expand into home care because, they believed, everyone would opt to receive care at home if he or she could. Nevertheless, insurers began creating products that covered home care when it was followed by a nursing home stay. This post-recovery benefit allowed insurers to gain experience with home care, and they soon realized that people don't abuse the benefit. Insurers learned that few people want to have strangers come into their homes to help them bathe, dress and use the toilet.

As a result, policies started covering home care without any prior institutionalization requirement. The availability of home care benefits allowed companies to honestly call this product *long-term care insurance*.

The 1990s saw an expansion in providers and insurers embracing LTC alternatives. Assisted-living facilities were added to nursing home policies to create nursing facility coverage. Adult day care centers and respite care services were added to home care and LTC insurance. Today, companies include alternate plan of care benefits to allow policy benefits to expand as the provider community continues to evolve.

■ GUARANTEED RENEWABLE

As LTC insurance products evolved, insurance companies began to take more risks. The pioneers in this business offered conditionally renewable nursing home insurance, just like automobile insurance. If claims became excessive or a company wanted out of the business for some other reason, it had the legal right to cancel all policyholders' coverage.

Informed consumers recognized this limitation and purchased only guaranteed renewable coverage. The insurers cannot cancel these policies, nor require insureds to provide evidence of insurability to renew the policies. Many other consumers were willing to forego the guarantee of renewability and to trust the insurance companies to keep the coverage in force. Some of these contracts may have been

ILL. 2.4 ■ *The Care Continuum*

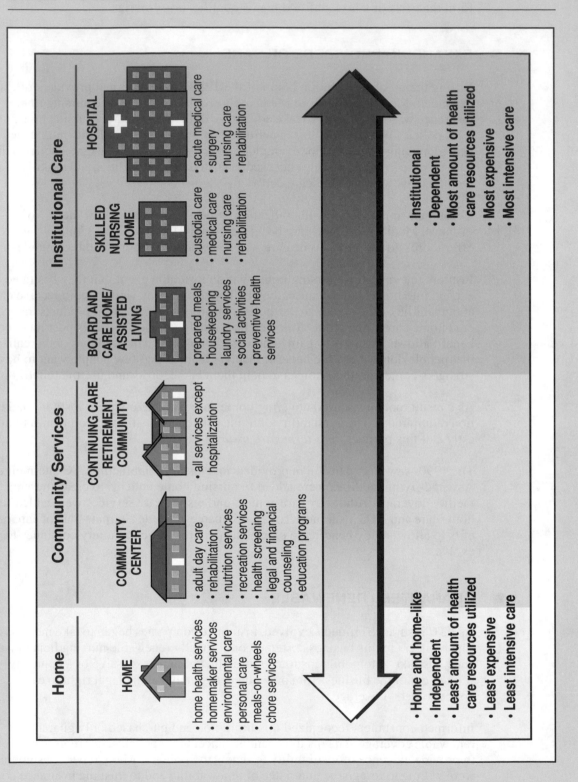

Home

HOME
- home health services
- homemaker services
- environmental care
- personal care
- meals-on-wheels
- chore services

Community Services

COMMUNITY CENTER
- adult day care
- rehabilitation
- nutrition services
- recreation services
- health screening
- legal and financial counseling
- education programs

CONTINUING CARE RETIREMENT COMMUNITY
- all services except hospitalization

Institutional Care

BOARD AND CARE HOME/ ASSISTED LIVING
- prepared meals
- housekeeping
- laundry services
- social activities
- preventive health services

SKILLED NURSING HOME
- custodial care
- medical care
- nursing care
- rehabilitation

HOSPITAL
- acute medical care
- surgery
- nursing care
- rehabilitation

- Home and home-like
- Independent
- Least amount of health care resources utilized
- Least expensive
- Least intensive care

- Institutional
- Dependent
- Most amount of health care resources utilized
- Most expensive
- Most intensive care

canceled, but eventually most companies offered their insureds an opportunity to convert to guaranteed renewable contracts. The savvy consumer took advantage of this generous offer.

What many consumers were not told (or didn't understand) when they purchased their coverage is that the premium for a guaranteed renewable contract can be raised or lowered. The term *level premiums,* used to explain the renewability clause, implied the premiums would not increase as a person aged, as with term life insurance. Consumers may have been told premiums could be adjusted for a class of insureds only—no individual could be singled out for a premium change. It is evident today that insureds didn't understand that the word *guaranteed* in the term *guaranteed renewable* referred to renewability only; it had nothing to do with the premium. A guaranteed premium contract is classified as *noncancelable.*

Then and now, insurers need the ability to adjust premiums. The data used for pricing the risk that insureds would need LTC were based on an entire population, not the insured population. This created doubt about the accuracy of pricing assumptions. An insured population is normally healthier (underwriting eliminates those who are most likely to need care in the foreseeable future), but people with insurance did not have the financial disincentive to enter an LTC facility. How they would react to entering one was unknown.

Another reason companies needed then, and still need now, the ability to adjust premiums was that the risks were changing as fast as LTC services and settings were evolving. Insurers may have known something about Medicare-certified skilled nursing facilities, but they understood nothing about custodial care facilities. Would the stigma of going to an "old folks home" attach itself to facilities that provided less intensive care than skilled nursing homes—like custodial care facilities? How to price a product that covered professional care in an insured's home also was a complete unknown. And no one had even heard of assisted-living facilities 15 years ago.

Today, we're finding out that some companies used assumptions in their pricing during the 1980s that were too aggressive for the way they did business. The worst-case scenario became reality for at least one company.

What is the worst thing that can happen? As claim costs exceed original projections, premiums are increased for a class of insureds. When premiums are raised, some of the healthy insureds let their coverage lapse and purchase new coverage from other companies. (The more the premiums increase, the more lapses occur. Actuaries call this *shock lapse rate.*) This puts additional pressure on the pool of insureds because the company does not have as many healthy people paying premiums. Another premium increase follows, and more of the healthy insureds replace their coverage with policies from different companies. As this process continues, the company and insureds experience a rate spiral, where the premium increases seem never ending and most of the remaining risk pool is uninsurable with other companies.

Fortunately for everyone involved in the long-term care insurance industry, few companies have this problem. The vast majority of insurers have been able to maintain stable pricing, and at least one has actually lowered premiums a couple of times.

The worst-case scenario draws the attention of those concerned with suitability because of the one company that went through a rate spiral before selling its block of long-term care insurance. No one wants to see this repeated. Therefore, additional disclosure by agents to consumers is necessary.

What ever happened to this block of business? A class action lawsuit was brought against the insurer and one of the insurance agencies that sold policies. The basis for the suit was that the applicants were told by the agents that the policies were level premium policies when, in fact, they were guaranteed renewable policies. Millions of dollars changed hands as a result of semantics. In a suitable sale, the agent explains the concept of guaranteed renewable to the applicant and never uses the term level premiums.

■ INFLATION PROTECTION

Consumer advocates in the late 1980s became sensitive to the fact that the value of policies being purchased would erode because of increasing costs. A common daily maximum then was $60 per day; a big sale was $100. Today, that doesn't come close to covering the cost of care in many metropolitan areas of the country.

Advocates in conjunction with regulators adopted standards for inflation protection. The original intent was to ensure that all policies included a feature that increased benefits by 5 percent, compounded annually. Insurers complained this would add significantly to the cost of the coverage and make LTC insurance unaffordable for most people.

Both regulators and insurers were right in their concerns. Since 1987, nursing home costs have increased by just about 5 percent, compounded annually. Offering inflation protection in LTC coverage did add to costs, doubling the premiums for younger people. However, those who added the feature have found its cost-effectiveness well worth the initial pain in purchasing it.

■ MEDICARE SUPPLEMENT INSURANCE AND THE RISE OF MARKET CONDUCT

Today's market conduct concerns stem from previous insurance sales practices to seniors. During the late 1980s, sales of Medicare-supplement insurance grew rapidly. The sales were relatively simple—find the people who wanted to minimize their out-of-pocket medical expenses and sell them policies they could afford. So much publicity leading up to the passage of the Medicare Catastrophic Health Care Act detailed the limitations of Medicare that seniors thought they had to have the best Medicare-supplement policies available. Sales of LTC policies increased also because in selling Medicare-supplement policies, agents had an opportunity to point out the inadequacy of Medicare and Medicare-supplement insurance in covering LTC costs.

Some agents sold these prospects new Medicare-supplement policies every year. The agents received high first-year commissions for the sales. Consumers were not harmed as long as they remained insurable and premiums remained relatively constant. However, insurers found that they never recovered their initial costs (underwriting, systems and commissions) in gaining new insureds. Under normal

ILL. 2.5 ■ *Medicare Supplement Plans*

A	B	C	D	E	F	G	H	I	J
Basic Benefits*	Basic Benefits	Basic Benefits	Basic Benefits	Basic Benefits	Basic Benefits	Basic Benefits	Basic Benefits	Basic Benefits	Basic Benefits
		Skilled Nursing Copayment	Skilled Nursing Copayment	Skilled Nursing Copayment	Skilled Nursing Copayment	Skilled Nursing Copayment	Skilled Nursing Copayment	Skilled Nursing Copayment	Skilled Nursing Copayment
	Part A Deductible	Part A Deductible	Part A Deductible	Part A Deductible	Part A Deductible	Part A Deductible	Part A Deductible	Part A Deductible	Part A Deductible
		Part B Deductible			Part B Deductible				Part B Deductible
					Part B Excess (100%)	Part B Excess (80%)		Part B Excess (100%)	Part B Excess (100%)
		Foreign Travel Emergency	Foreign Travel Emergency	Foreign Travel Emergency	Foreign Travel Emergency	Foreign Travel Emergency	Foreign Travel Emergency	Foreign Travel Emergency	Foreign Travel Emergency
			At-Home Recovery			At-Home Recovery		At-Home Recovery	At-Home Recovery
							Basic Drugs ($1,250 Limit)	Basic Drugs ($1,250 Limit)	Extended Drugs ($3,000 Limit)
				Preventive Care					Preventive Care

Source: National Association of Insurance Commissioners.

*The basic benefits consist of coverage for the Part A coinsurance amount for the 61st through the 90th day of hospitalization in each Medicare benefit period; coverage for the Part A coinsurance amount for each of the 60 lifetime reserve days; coverage for 100% of Part A hospital expenses after all Medicare hospital benefits have been exhausted, subject to a lifetime maximum benefit of an additional 365 days; coverage under both parts A and B for the reasonable cost of the first three pints of blood; and coverage for the 20% copayments under Medicare Part B.

circumstances, they recaptured these costs in renewal years. Thus, insurers had to increase rates on Medicare-supplement coverage.

The following steps were taken to discourage this practice:

- Companies had to report to state insurance departments their experience with agents who experienced high levels of replacement activity.

- Agents who replaced policies received lower renewal commissions.

- Agents had to make additional disclosure when replacing Medicare-supplement policies.

Another problem was that consumers were so frightened of having to spend their retirement nest eggs on needed medical treatment that they purchased Medicare-supplement policies that covered every conceivable risk. However, no company offered a perfect policy, so few agents sold multiple Medicare-supplement policies. Every time a new feature or option was added, they sold their clients new policies without instructing them to lapse their existing coverage. (Remember, agents received reduced compensation for replacement, and, therefore, had a financial incentive for not providing this important advice.) As a result, consumers wasted their money on duplicate coverage. Getting a routine claim paid was a paperwork nightmare—for the consumer, the care provider and the multiple insurance companies.

To reduce the number of Medicare-supplement policies being offered for sale and to eliminate some of the questionable marketing practices associated with these policies, Congress passed a far-reaching Medigap law that required the National Association of Insurance Commissioners (NAIC) to address the subject. Specifically, the NAIC's task was to develop a standardized model Medicare-supplement policy that provided certain core benefits, plus as many as nine other supplement policies that provided increasingly more comprehensive benefits. Ten model policies, labeled A through J, were developed and adopted by states as prototype policies for their insurers. It was intended that these model policies would help consumers better understand Medicare-supplement policies, thereby allowing them to make more informed buying decisions by:

- standardizing coverages and benefits from one policy to the next;

- simplifying the terms used in these policies;

- facilitating policy comparisons; and

- eliminating policy provisions that may be misleading or confusing.

In addition, agent compensation became the same regardless of how long a policy has been in force. States scrutinized marketing materials for misleading information, and disclosure requirements at the time of sale were expanded. No longer was there a need to own more than one Medicare-supplement plan, and the financial incentive to replace coverage regularly was eliminated.

■ REGULATING LTC INSURANCE

The painful learning experience in designing and selling LTC insurance created the need for regulations addressing suitability, product disclosure and sales practices. Today, LTC insurance is probably the third most regulated industry in America—right behind nuclear power and nursing homes. Companies must submit all of the following documents to state insurance departments:

- policy;

- actuarial memorandum outlining the assumptions used in establishing the rates;

- application;

- all disclosure documentation including the outline of coverage and suitability disclosure; and

- all advertising materials, including brochures, print ads, seminars, letters and so forth.

The NAIC has developed both a model act and model regulation for LTC policies that attempt to balance a consumer's interests with an insurance company's ability to market quality coverage successfully. The NAIC model act and regulation give state insurance departments a basis for developing rules governing LTC insurance. These documents address many aspects of LTC insurance, including—but not limited to—the following:

- incontestability period

- nonforfeiture benefits

- administrative procedures

- penalties

- policy definitions

- unintentional lapse

- required disclosure provisions

- prohibition against post-claims underwriting

- standards for home care benefits

- requirement to offer inflation protection

- requirements for applications and replacements

- reporting requirements

- reserve standards

- loss ratios

- filing requirements

- standards for marketing

- suitability

ILL. 2.6 ■ *Amount of TQ Policy Premium Treatable as Medical Expense*

The following amounts of TQ policy premium are the maximum that can be included with other unreimbursed medical expenses in 1999.* If a couple files a joint return, these amounts are per person.

Age	Amount
40 or younger	$210
41–50	$400
51–60	$800
61–70	$2,120
71 and older	$2,660

*This amount will be indexed for inflation.

- standards for benefit triggers

- requirement to deliver the shopper's guide

Both the model act and regulation are dynamic documents, revised and updated constantly to address new and emerging issues. Today, the NAIC is giving serious consideration to adding regulations to discourage insurers from underpricing their products and later being forced to increase rates dramatically.

Today's products are either tax-qualified (TQ) or nontax-qualified (NTQ) policies. TQ policies are designed to meet the standards set forth in the Health Insurance Portability and Accountability Act of 1996 (HIPAA). This landmark legislation for long-term care insurance clarified how insureds should treat premiums and benefits when completing their taxes. An unexpected consequence of the tax clarification was the standards established for TQ policies.

A taxpayer can include the premium for a TQ policy with his or her unreimbursed medical expenses. Unreimbursed medical expenses are deductible once they exceed 7.5 percent of adjusted gross income. Given the fact that the average senior spends 19 percent of his or her income on medical expenses (the percentage is higher for those with Medicare-supplement insurance), this can help make LTC insurance more affordable. The amount of premium that can be included with unreimbursed medical expenses is based on an insured's age, as outlined in Ill. 2.6.

The benefits a person receives from a TQ plan generally are considered free from taxation. Each LTC claimant receives Form 1099-LTC from the insurer. This form instructs the recipient to complete Form 8853 to determine the extent of the tax-free benefits. These forms can be examined in Appendix C. While the forms answer many questions clearly, they don't answer other questions. For example, one

ILL. 2.7 ■ *Benefit Triggers for Tax-Qualified Benefits*

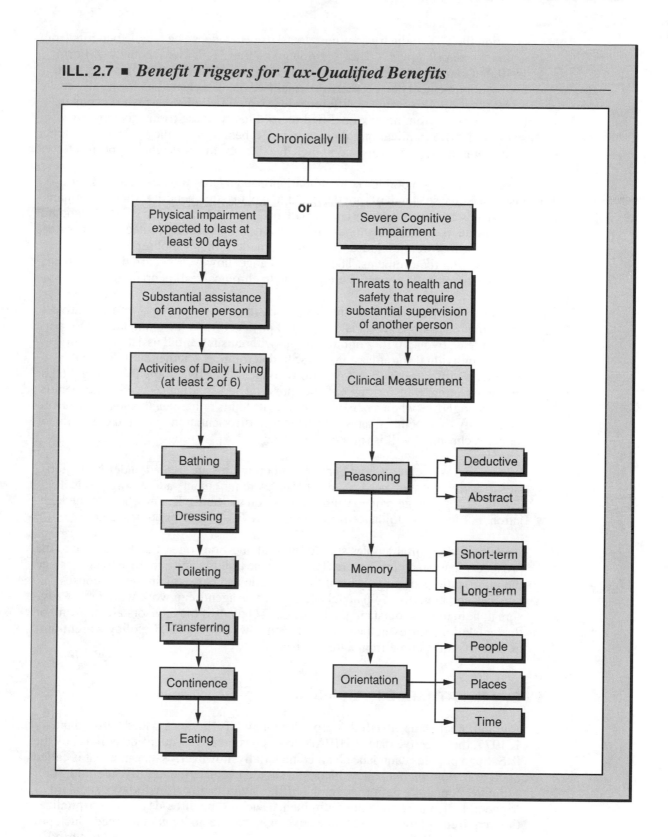

question the LTC industry continues to ask is "How does one handle benefits from a nontax-qualified plan?" They seem to go on line 21, "other income," of Form 1040, but some people disagree with this interpretation. Handling benefits from both reimbursement and per diem tax-qualified plans is clear. The forms also make it clear that the IRS wants to differentiate tax-qualified plans, which it prints in bold-face type, from nontax-qualified plans. Finally, these forms give agents a sense of the IRS implications of receiving LTC benefits, and they help agents direct their claimants to the forms and knowledgeable tax advisors when appropriate.

In return for the favorable tax treatment, more standards were established for LTC insurance. These standards are designed to pay tax-free benefits when a claimant truly needs care from appropriate providers. The regulations stop short of standardizing products and eliminating future innovations. Consumer protection measures, many of which were included in the NAIC models, must be observed, as well as new reporting requirements. The biggest change, however, occurred in how benefits are triggered. TQ benefits are payable to chronically ill people only.

The term chronically ill is defined as possessing either a physical or a cognitive impairment. An impairment is considered physical when the claimant cannot perform at least two activities of daily living without substantial assistance from another individual for at least 90 days. In determining whether an individual is chronically ill, a policy must take into account at least five of the following ADLs: eating, toileting, transferring, bathing, dressing and continence. An impairment is deemed cognitive when a person poses threats to his or her health and safety due to an inability to remember, a loss of memory or disorientation. A visual definition of the term chronically ill is shown in Illustration 2.7

What remains unclear is how benefits and premiums are treated under NTQ policies. It is evident they need not meet HIPAA requirements addressing product design, benefit triggers or consumer protection measures. But nowhere in the legislation, tax forms or guidance from the IRS are NTQ policies addressed.

Agents making suitable sales should refer all questions regarding tax advice to the prospects' personal tax advisors. They have the training and expertise to understand the ramifications of all aspects of the IRS code and can explain the tax consequences and benefits of financial decisions. The agents can work with the tax advisors to help them understand the impact of TQ plans if the advisors are unaware of the legislation; however, the final advice on how to treat an LTC policy's premiums or benefits must come from a tax advisor.

■ GRANDFATHERED POLICIES

A grandfather clause in HIPAA provides for all LTC policies issued before January 1, 1977, the effective date of HIPAA, to be considered tax-qualified policies by the IRS. Such policies cannot be changed materially, however. When an agent is called upon to review such a policy, he or she should evaluate it carefully. It could, for example, contain benefit triggers that differ significantly from today's standard triggers. It also may contain requirements, such as the three-day prior hospitalization requirement for nursing home coverage, that are no longer enforced. Such policies should be left in force unless significant premium increases have occurred, which may be the case because older age means higher premiums.

▪ SUMMARY

LTC insurance products have evolved from highly restrictive nursing home-only coverage that mirrored Medicare's benefit triggers to a variety of plans that reflect the needs and desires of the recipients of LTC services. For example, benefits have been extended beyond LTC facilities to cover care in the home and in new and emerging settings in the community. Today's LTC policies, whether they be tax-qualified or nontax-qualified, offer considerable flexibility and a variety of policy features and options. However, the products are still relatively new to most prospects and remain complex. To make sales suitable, agents must educate clients and provide full and accurate disclosure. When a prospect has an existing policy, it is best to consider it a foundation to build upon. Only an educated prospect can select options and purchase an LTC policy that meets his or her LTC needs.

▪ CHAPTER 2 QUESTIONS FOR REVIEW

1. All of the following statements are true of guaranteed renewable coverage EXCEPT

    A. the policy can't be canceled

    B. evidence of insurability is not required for renewal

    C. premiums can't be raised

    D. only renewability is guaranteed

2. Which of the following is NOT a qualification for benefits in the original nursing home insurance policies?

    A. Spend three days in a hospital

    B. Enter a Medicare-certified skilled nursing facility

    C. Be chronically ill

    D. Receive skilled nursing care

3. What is the term used to describe the following phenomenon: the greater the premium increase, the more lapses occur?

    A. Spiraling premium effect

    B. Shock lapse rate

    C. High/low lapse phenomenon

    D. Soaring lapse scales

4. Which of the following is NOT one of the reasons for the dramatic rise in the need for LTC insurance?

    A. Rising cost of health care

    B. Budgets of outside payment sources, which are stretched thin

    C. Strength of the US economy in the 90s

    D. Fact that people are living longer lives

5. The average annual cost of nursing home care in the United States increases by about what percentage every year?

A. 3 percent

B. 5 percent

C. 7 percent

D. 10 percent

Introducing Clients to Long-Term Care

A gents who sell long-term care insurance meet many prospects. Some have had personal experiences with LTC, while others have not. Many have heard stories of those who suffered financial disaster because they had to pay for the costs of extended stays in nursing homes out of their own pockets. However, when it comes to LTC insurance, most people know nothing about it, and those who do have some understanding usually also have many misconceptions. Few prospects have extensive accurate knowledge of LTC insurance. In fact, most prospects' first exposure to LTC insurance happens at the first meetings with their agents.

A prospect who agrees to meet with an agent to talk about LTC insurance is expressing an interest in learning about the topic. The agent's challenge is to get to know the prospect well enough to tailor a presentation to the prospect's level of knowledge and circumstances.

There is no best way to explain the need for LTC insurance to a prospect. Successful agents master a system, then adapt it to suit their personalities and beliefs about the subject. They don't assume their prospects understand what LTC is or who pays for it. This assumption would be a mistake because so many people think they understand these topics but don't. Many popular myths and half-truths surround LTC and LTC insurance.

This chapter presents a methodical approach to discussing LTC insurance. The system is proven, honest, factual and suitable. Experienced agents representing different companies in various parts of the country use it successfully, as can agents with less insurance sales experience who are interested in entering the LTC market.

The first step is to introduce prospects to long-term care. Few understand what composes LTC. Explaining long-term care provides a foundation of knowledge upon which to build as agents work with prospects.

■ ■ ■ ■ ■

■   BUILDING THE FOUNDATION

People should plan for long-term care with knowledgeable professionals. LTC and LTC insurance are complex and difficult because they possess their own jargon that people outside the industry don't use. Furthermore, LTC insurance, in particular, is steeped in myth and misinformation. The guidance of a professional who has a client's best interests at heart is essential. Discussions about LTC get into sensitive areas that can be quite emotional for clients. For example, an agent may try to create some doubt about the ability, if not the willingness, of children to care for their parents. Such a topic must be handled with the utmost delicacy. Agents can adapt the following material to introduce prospects to LTC and provide foundations upon which to build suitable LTC insurance policies.

Most people have vague notions that their children will care for them when the time comes. And it is true that most LTC is provided by family. However, even when family members are willing and able, providing such care creates physical, emotional and financial stress. It is difficult to help someone for long periods of time. The caregiver must balance his or her personal needs with those of the care recipient, who eventually may demand constant attention.

When people begin to lose their independence and need help with ordinary activities, family and friends usually step in and provide the needed assistance. This is called *informal care,* in contrast to the formal care provided by health care professionals. About three-quarters of this type of care delivered in the United States is provided by family and friends—those individuals who love the person so much they're willing to sacrifice to care for him or her. However, we now know from research and personal experience that the caregiving role is demanding and stressful. Caregivers often don't have the skills, time or resources to provide the assistance that is needed.

Physical stress can come from having to be with, watch over or move a person—for example, from a bed to a chair. When such stress is prolonged and the caregiver doesn't take time out for personal activities, he or she can experience physical exhaustion easily.

Emotional stress arises from watching a loved one deteriorate physically or mentally. Like physical stress, emotional stress can become exhausting when it's prolonged, with little or no relief. While caregiving is expensive in terms of physical and emotional stress, it's also financially expensive. Some caregivers work fewer hours; some replace their full-time positions with part-time employment; and some even quit their jobs. Expenses increase as people try to pay in both time and money for their loved ones' care. The financial stress arises because most adults can't afford the added expenses when they are trying to raise their families and plan for their own retirements. As all this stress builds, caregivers look for help elsewhere.

Home Health Care and Community Services

Because most people needing care want to stay at home as long as possible, the first recourse is usually community-based services. Often, community services, such as meals on wheels and transportation services, are available to supplement caregivers' abilities and time constraints. A care recipient can stay at home longer if his or her caregiver can get help from a home health care agency or an adult day care

---

ILL. 3.1 ■ *Facts to Ponder about Long-Term Care*

Misinformation about LTC and LTC insurance abounds. A 1996 survey, conducted by John Hancock Mutual Life Insurance Company and the National Council on Aging to investigate knowledge and attitudes about long-term care, demonstrates some preconceived notions agents may face.

- While 84 percent of those surveyed were familiar with nursing homes, half of them are unacquainted with other LTC options, including adult day care, retirement communities and assisted living facilities.
- Eighty-six percent of those surveyed did not realize that most LTC (80 percent, in fact) is provided in the recipients' homes.
- Only 10 percent had an accurate picture of their own risk of needing LTC.
- People aren't sure what kind of policy covers LTC. In fact, 11 percent of those surveyed thought they were covered for long-term care when only 3 percent actually were.
- Many people think Medicare or Medicaid pays for chronic care; 48 percent of those surveyed did not know that people must spend practically all their assets to get Medicaid benefits.
- Most people don't want to think about long-term care.
- Of those surveyed, 88 percent believed that providing LTC for older or disabled people is a major problem, but 89 percent didn't own any LTC coverage.
- Sixty percent of those surveyed reported having family or friends who have needed LTC.
- Fifty-six percent have done minimal planning for their LTC, and 66 percent have not made it a priority.
- Of those surveyed, 69 percent reported they find it difficult even to admit they might need LTC, and nearly 40 percent said they would rather deal with LTC if and when it happened.

---

center. A home health care agency can come in for a couple of hours each day to provide assistance with personal hygiene or to offer medical services or therapies. An adult day care center could provide assistance during the day while the family member tends to other responsibilities, such as working or managing the household. Home care agencies provide limited health services and offer social interaction, light housekeeping and meals for the elderly.

Agents can use Ill. 3.3 to show clients how care providers interact with one another to keep a loved one in the community. The illustration assumes that as part of the aging process, a person has developed a chronic condition and needs care from family and friends and from professionals in organized health care settings and the community. This scenario reinforces the fact that people today are living longer than ever before and, as a result, need more care than families can provide. Eventually, they may need to seek care in a nursing facility.

ILL. 3.2 ■ *Informal Caregivers in The United States*

More than 25 million informal caregivers live in the United States. The time these caregivers dedicate is worth between $45 billion and $75 billion a year. The following statistics describe this segment of the population:

- Just more than half of all caregivers (52 percent) work full time.
- Of caregivers who hold jobs while providing care, more than half have made changes at work to accommodate the caregiving. Common adjustments include going in late, leaving early and taking time off.
- Caregivers spend an average of 18 hours a week providing care.
- Of caregivers who provide 40 hours or more of care a week, 30 percent are at least 65 years old.
- The average duration of caregiving is 4½ years
- Seventy-three percent of caregivers are female; care recipients are typically female relatives.
- The average caregiver is 46 years old. Twenty-two percent are younger than age 35, and 12 percent are 65 years and older.
- The average age of care recipients is 77 years. Forty percent of care recipients are older than age 75. Twenty-four percent are older than age 85.
- Seventy-one percent of care recipients suffer from long-term chronic conditions, and another 11 percent suffer from short-term chronic conditions.
- Thirty-one percent of all caregivers say they have experienced physical or mental problems because of caregiving.
- Caregivers cope by praying, talking with friends or relatives, exercising and continuing their hobbies.

Sources: National Family Caregivers Association; Administration on Aging; and from Family Caregiving in the U.S.: Findings from a National Survey, sponsored by the National Alliance for Caregiving and the American Association of Retired Persons.

LTC Nursing Facilities

Eventually, the best place for many elderly people to receive the full-time care they require is an LTC nursing facility, a health care setting organized and staffed to meet their needs. Here, they have access to trained health care professionals, often including physicians, on duty for treatments and therapy. Such facilities also provide social activities, such as day trips to local attractions. Many people that enter LTC nursing facilities develop new networks of friends and engage in social activities with their peers. They discover new sources of enjoyment that simply are not available to them living alone at home.

Each year, it becomes increasingly important to plan for the possibility of needing nursing home care. Every year, people live longer lives. Since 1900, the number of Americans 65 and over has increased 11 times, from 3.1 million to 34.1 million. Furthermore, the older population continues to grow rapidly. It will burgeon between 2010 and 2030 as the baby boomers reach age 65.

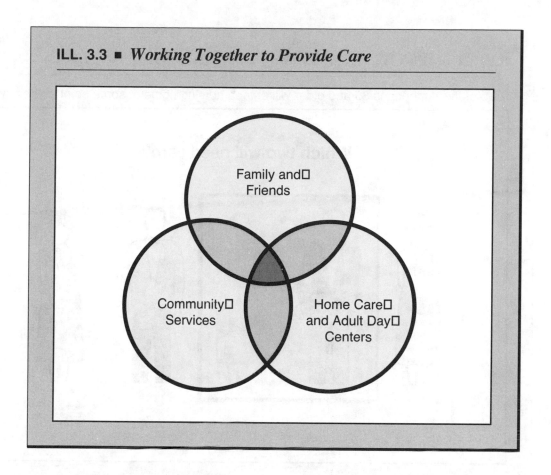

ILL. 3.3 ■ *Working Together to Provide Care*

Family and□
Friends

Community□
Services

Home Care□
and Adult Day□
Centers

A definitive study published in the *New England Journal of Medicine* in 1991 estimated that about 43 percent of Americans 65 years and older would enter nursing homes at some time in their lives. Many people believe they never will need care in a facility, and that hope may prove true. Nevertheless, a 65-year-old faces odds that are better than two out of five that he or she will be admitted to a nursing home. These odds increase as people age. All this means is that more and more people will need LTC services either at home or in LTC nursing facilities.

When agents discuss these statistics with clients—and probably the 2-out-of-5 statistic for people older than age 65 will be the easiest for clients to understand—some prospects will think the probability of needing LTC is high and others will recognize the odds as less than 50-50. For the latter individuals, agents should focus on what can be lost in paying for LTC rather than on the odds of losing it. It's also worth mentioning that such statistics merely give us insight into what may happen to the population at large. They do not indicate what will happen to individuals. Nevertheless, these figures and statistics are helpful in educating clients to the realities of LTC.

Advising clients to consider and plan for their LTC needs is not an idle recommendation. Consider the benefits of planning for long-term care. Clients enjoy peace of mind knowing that they will be able to maintain their independence and not become burdens to their children. That peace of mind also encompasses knowing that their income and assets are protected, that any valuables they wish to leave to their heirs

ILL. 3.4 ■ *Who Will Need Nursing Home Care?*

Two of five Americans 65 and older will enter a nursing home at some point in their lives.

Which two will need care?

are secure and that they will be able to maintain their dignity and pride. In addition, clients gain considerable freedom in selecting facilities where they wish to receive care, the health care professionals they want to provide it, as well as the social and other activities they'd like to be involved in.

Agents can use Illustration 3.5 when discussing length of stay in nursing homes; however, one drawback to using this illustration is that many prospects consider themselves average, so they focus on the average stay of 2.5 years. The point agents want to get across is that nursing home care is expensive, averaging $48,000 a year in 2000 and rising 5 percent annually. What is traumatic to an individual is the loss of dignity and pride involved in liquidating assets to pay for this costly care.

Once in nursing homes, people tend to live there for a long time. About one-third of those in nursing homes today have been there less than a year, about a third have lived there one to three years, while the balance has been there three or more years. Almost one in five has been living in a facility five or more years. Obviously, such stays can be financially devastating.

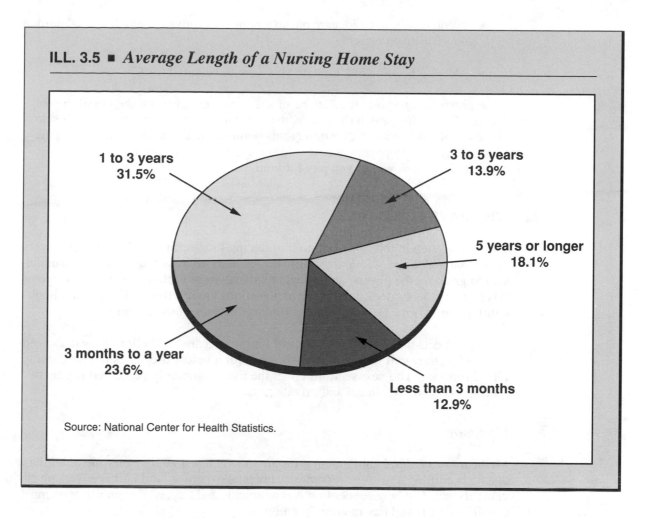

ILL. 3.5 ■ *Average Length of a Nursing Home Stay*

Source: National Center for Health Statistics.

■ **TALKING TO CLIENTS**

After discussing the probability of needing LTC, an agent should ask a prospect the following question: "Why do you think the chances of needing care are so high?" The agent should allow the prospect to identify and discuss some reasons, then continue with something like the following: "People today live different lives than people lived a few decades ago. They live longer, for one thing. Modern technology and medical science have done a great job treating acute conditions that used to kill people, such as heart attacks, strokes and cancer. But they haven't achieved the same success with chronic conditions. They can't cure arthritis, diabetes, hearing and vision impairments and other chronic conditions—though many treatments are available. Recovery from these conditions is unlikely."

At this point in the interview some agents ask difficult questions, intended to reinforce the lessons of the previous discussion. Some examples of questions they ask follow:

- "Given your family history, what are some of the likely things that could cause you to need care as you age?"

- "Would your need for care put an emotional, a physical or a financial burden on your loved ones?"

- "As you become old, how do you want to be cared for?"

If the prospect's answers indicate he or she is concerned about the possibility of needing long-term care in the future, the agent has a good opportunity for a sale. Some agents like to ask a question at this point of the discussion that transitions them into the likely payers of care—for example, "If you had to go to a nursing home tonight, how would you pay for your care?"

■ WHO PAYS FOR CARE?

The second step in this approach to introducing long-term care is to describe who pays what and when. While the following sections address the common misunderstandings about the payers, an in-depth explanation of each is beyond the scope of this text. Readers interested in such explanations are referred to Dearborn's book entitled *Long-Term Care* for more complete analyses of these options.

After prospects understand the basics of long-term care and believe they may need it someday, they will want to know who pays for it before they consider purchasing LTC insurance. The next sections cover the most commonly perceived payers of LTC—Medicare, Medicaid and private pay.

Medicare

Medicare is a federal entitlement program to which just about everyone older than age 65 is entitled. Part A covers mostly hospital expenses, and Part B covers physician services. Coverage under Part A is automatic and free, while beneficiaries must enroll in Part B and pay monthly premiums.

A popular myth agents must overcome is that Medicare pays for long-term care. The few people who realize it doesn't don't understand why. Agents can do a great service for prospects by explaining Medicare benefits. At the same time, the agents cement the trust they've established with the prospects.

Medicare was designed to cover hospital and physician costs associated with acute illnesses and injuries. It never was intended to cover chronic conditions that require LTC at home or in a nursing facility. Medicare pays for short, intensive stays in LTC facilities under very restrictive requirements.

Under Part A, Medicare's skilled nursing home benefits are available only if a person meets the following three conditions:

1. The patient must have been in the hospital for at least three consecutive days before entering the nursing home. Furthermore, the patient must be admitted to the nursing home within 30 days of discharge from the hospital.

2. A doctor must certify that skilled nursing is required.

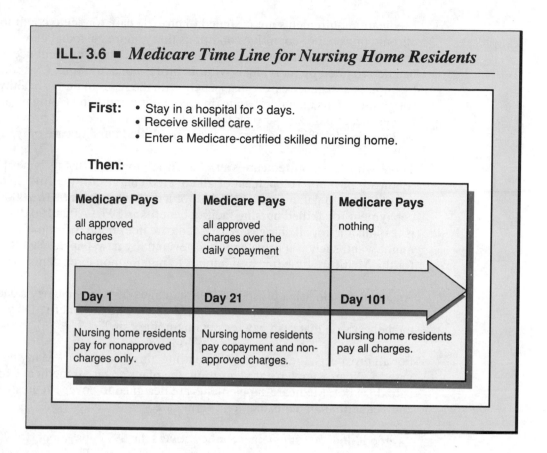

ILL. 3.6 ■ *Medicare Time Line for Nursing Home Residents*

First:
- Stay in a hospital for 3 days.
- Receive skilled care.
- Enter a Medicare-certified skilled nursing home.

Then:

Medicare Pays	**Medicare Pays**	**Medicare Pays**
all approved charges	all approved charges over the daily copayment	nothing
Day 1	**Day 21**	**Day 101**
Nursing home residents pay for nonapproved charges only.	Nursing home residents pay copayment and non-approved charges.	Nursing home residents pay all charges.

   3. The services or care must be provided by a Medicare-certified skilled
      nursing facility.

As a result of these requirements, the number of nursing home stays covered by
Medicare is quite limited. To begin with, only about half of the people who enter
nursing homes have been in hospitals previously. Furthermore, coverage for most
chronic and cognitive impairments is ruled out because the nursing home care must
be for the same condition for which hospital care was needed. Chronic conditions
and cognitive impairments typically do not require hospital stays before nursing
home care is required. In addition, patients must enter Medicare-certified skilled
nursing facilities. Not all nursing homes are skilled nursing homes, and not all
skilled nursing homes are Medicare certified. Many facilities do not want the paperwork burden Medicare imposes on nursing homes that want to obtain and maintain
certification.

The requirement that a patient must receive skilled nursing care further restricts
Medicare's coverage. Skilled care is the most intensive type of care delivered outside a hospital. A nurse, under a doctor's orders, visits the patient every day, and
the patient must show signs of continuous recovery from his or her ailment. Skilled
care is administered for short periods of time, rarely lasting longer than four weeks.
For this reason, Medicare does not cover treatment for arthritis, Alzheimer's disease
and other chronic conditions common to old age. People do not recover from these
continuing ailments, and thus, they don't receive skilled care for treatment.

Medicare requirements are designed to provide care for acute conditions—not chronic physical or cognitive conditions that require custodial care. Care is considered custodial when it meets personal needs rather than medical needs or when it can be provided by individuals without professional training. Custodial care is essentially assistance care—that is, help with the types of things healthy people take for granted. This includes getting dressed, taking baths and eating meals. In nursing homes, custodial care is by far the most common type of care provided. Medicare will not pay for this type of care; it covers skilled nursing care only.

Those who do meet Medicare's strict qualifications find that its benefits are limited. Medicare pays for 100 percent of all covered charges for the first 20 days. For the next 80 days, a patient is responsible for a daily copayment. (In 2000, the daily copayment for skilled nursing facility benefits is $97.) After 100 days, the patient is responsible for all charges. Also, Medicare does not pay for many items a patient might want, such as a private room or even daily newspapers. See Illustration 3.6 for the Medicare time line as it applies to nursing home residents.

An agent should ask a prospect older than age 65, "Do you carry a Medicare-supplement plan? Does it include the skilled nursing home benefit? Do you know how the benefits on that plan pay for nursing home care?"

For all prospects, the agent should continue this discussion: "Many people with private Medicare-supplement plans think the plans cover all medical expenses Medicare does not. Medicare supplements are designed to cover Medicare copayment and deductible amounts, not long-term care.

"A good Medicare supplement policy covers the $97 copayment (for 2000), but that is all most Medicare supplements are designed to pay. They cover Medicare copayments and deductibles on expenses covered by Medicare. They normally do not pay for treatments Medicare does not cover—such as skilled care after the 100th day and custodial care."

Medicaid

In discussing Medicaid with prospects, it is best to address the following issues:

- qualification process

- quality of care issue

- asset recovery program

Medicaid is a joint federal and state means-tested program. (Many people think of Medicaid as an "entitlement program," like Medicare, but it is a means-tested program, like food stamps.) To qualify for benefits, applicants must show they don't have the financial means to pay for their own care. The government evaluates their assets and income to determine whether they qualify for Medicaid.

The federal government sets broad qualification guidelines that states administer. State governments can adjust the requirements to make it more difficult to qualify for benefits. States are not supposed to make their requirements less stringent than federal standards, yet some do.

ILL. 3.7 ■ *Medicaid's Financial Requirements*

Completing a simple graphic such as this one will dramatically illustrate the effects of relying on Medicaid to finance nursing home care.

Assets		Income
$ _____	**community spouse**	$ _____
$ _____	**nursing home resident**	$ _____

County governments administer the qualification process in most states. The qualification criteria can vary by county, and some caseworkers are more stringent than others. As a result, no single set of requirements is used consistently in each locale.

An agent should meet with a Medicaid caseworker in the agent's area. Traveling to the office gives the agent a feeling for what people go through in applying for Medicaid benefits. Many states make excellent brochures available at Medicaid offices explaining the program and how to qualify for benefits. Also, the agent should study an application form to better understand the extent of information that must be disclosed. The agent should ask about the area's asset and income requirements that a person must meet to qualify for Medicaid.

An applicant must spend down in four categories to qualify for Medicaid:

1. nursing home resident's assets

2. nursing home resident's income

3. community spouse's assets

4. community spouse's income

Some states do not have income qualification criteria. Those that do assess an applicant's income using a formula that combines a maximum and minimum allowed, with an additional allowance for housing expenses. An agent should ask a caseworker to explain the formula.

Another important piece of the Medicaid qualification puzzle is the personal needs allowance. This is the amount of income a nursing home resident can keep to pay for expenses that are not covered, such as haircuts, clothing, newspapers and magazines, and long-distance phone calls. An agent should inquire about the nursing home resident's personal needs allowance.

The agent also should ask a Medicaid caseworker to explain the qualification process. Many caseworkers realize the insurance option is an excellent alternative to the humbling asset liquidation process people go through to qualify for Medicaid. Therefore, experienced caseworkers often are willing and able to answer all of an agent's questions.

The agent, in his or her discussions with prospects, should discuss Medicaid's financial requirements. A typical explanation might go something like this: "The other government program that pays for nursing home care is Medicaid. Medicaid is a joint federal and state means-tested program. The federal government sets broad guidelines, then each state designs and administers the program based on local needs, state budget constraints and standards of living. Medicaid, unlike Medicare, does pay for custodial care in a nursing home. However, there are some distinct disadvantages to using Medicaid to cover these costs.

"To qualify in your state (or county), your income cannot exceed $_____ per month, and your assets must be less than $_____. For people with more than the maximum income or assets, the excess must be spent down to the allowable level to receive benefits. Not even partial benefits are paid until both the income and assets are less than the maximum allowed.

"For personal items Medicaid does not cover, such as toothpaste, clothes, magazines, long-distance phone calls and birthday cards to the grandchildren, a $_____ monthly personal needs allowance is provided.

"If your spouse stays healthy and remains in the community, he or she can keep $_____ in assets and an additional $_____ per month in income.

"Your house is excluded from the assets under special circumstances. If your doctor certifies you will return to it within six months of your nursing home admission, you can keep it. Your spouse can stay in it, as can a disabled child. There is also a special exemption for a brother or sister with an ownership interest or a child who cared for you for a couple of years.

"Once on Medicaid, you must receive care in a Medicaid-certified care facility. If Medicaid beds are not available in this area, you will be sent to the nearest available Medicaid bed. That may be in _____ (a town nearby) or _____ (another town nearby.)

"Keep in mind the state's Medicaid payment to the nursing home does not always cover the total cost of care. When this happens, some nursing homes are forced to:

- reduce the expenses of providing care;

- charge the private pay residents more to subsidize the Medicaid residents;

- refuse to accept more Medicaid patients; and

- go out of business.

"The federal government now requires each state to implement an estate recovery program. These programs try to recover funds from people with substantial resources who somehow managed to have Medicaid pay the cost of their long-term care. Because of the successful strategies they used, these people left sizable estates to their heirs. A state recovery program is designed to recover the money the state paid for a recipient's care from the recipient's estate or his or her spouse's estate. States also may recover money from trusts. Some states are more aggressive than others in their approach to the recovery process.

"Counties use the Medicaid application and support documents, including trusts and annuities, to find recoverable assets. When a Medicaid recipient dies, the state tracks down the new owner of an asset. The state can put a lien on the asset or force the new owner to sell it to pay the state's bill.

"Along with the qualification process, counties administer the recovery program. An agent can try to get a sense of the program while visiting a Medicaid office; however, it is likely that someone other than the qualification caseworker does the estate recovery work. The agent should ask to meet with the person handling estate recoveries."

The agent should continue the explanation of Medicaid's financial requirements: "Medicaid also can make things difficult for heirs. The state has the right to recover money paid for care from a recipient's children or anyone else who inherited money or assets.

"Needless to say, Medicaid is not a desirable option for people who have assets they want to pass to their loved ones and who want to maintain control of their options."

LTC coverage is not suitable for people qualified for Medicaid. They do not have enough income to pay the premiums and already have a payment source for their nursing home stays. The only time a sale could be suitable for someone on Medicaid is when the children pay the full premium. Agents are highly discouraged from making sales even in those rare instances, and most companies will not issue coverage to someone already on Medicaid.

Private Pay

Many people think they have enough money to pay for long-term care until they understand how much it costs for an extended stay in a nursing home. Some can afford to self-insure, but most Americans are at risk of liquidating or significantly depleting their estates when they have to pay for LTC out of pocket.

Illustration 3.8 shows prospects the costs of various lengths of stay at various daily costs in today's nursing facilities. As is evident, people can lose all of their hard-

ILL. 3.8 ■ *Lengths of Stay and Costs in Nursing Facilities*			
	1 year	**3 years**	**6 years**	**10 years**
$100/day	$36,500	$109,500	$219,000	$365,000
$150/day	$54,750	$164,250	$328,500	$547,500
$200/day	$73,000	$219,000	$438,000	$730,000
$250/day	$91,250	$273,750	$547,500	$912,500

earned savings and investments quickly. One of the primary reasons people purchase LTC insurance is to protect themselves from such financial loss. While the statistics show what can happen to a large group of people, the amount of potential loss indicated on this illustration is personal.

Two types of people are not good prospects for long-term care insurance:

1. people who have so much money that the costs shown in Illustration 3.8 would not dent their estates, although many wealthy people find that shifting the risk of paying for care to an insurance company is a prudent and logical decision; and

2. people who have so little money they probably qualify for Medicaid.

Everyone between *too rich* and *too poor* is a good prospect for LTC insurance.

Many agents adapt the following model presentation for their use:

"A good nursing home in this area costs about $_____(call several in the area to find out local costs). When you consider that the average length of a stay in a nursing home is almost three years, the cost is staggering—about $_____ in all. The picture is worse for conditions like Alzheimer's disease, which can easily last 6 years and may even extend to 10 years or more."

Using the chart in Illustration 3.8 or a similar one of his or her own devising, an agent should ask the prospect, "How long could you afford to pay for care, knowing these costs?" The agent should give the prospect a few moments to assess how much he or she has in assets. This is valuable information for the fact-finder, presented in the next chapter.

When the agent asks, "Do you want to spend your hard-earned retirement nest egg on a nursing home stay?" Most prospects will say no. If they say yes, a logical alternative for them is to use the interest earnings off some of their assets to pay the LTC insurance premium.

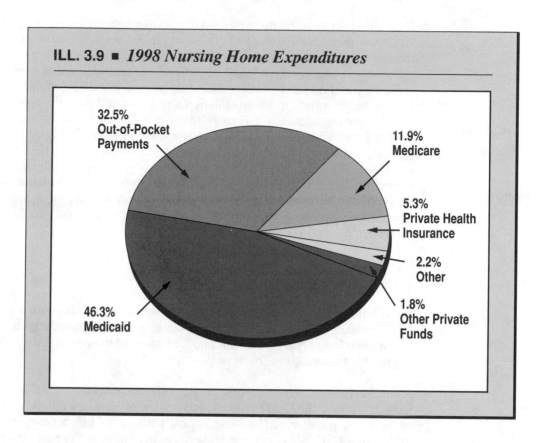

ILL. 3.9 ■ *1998 Nursing Home Expenditures*

32.5%
Out-of-Pocket
Payments

11.9%
Medicare

5.3%
Private Health
Insurance

2.2%
Other

1.8%
Other Private
Funds

46.3%
Medicaid

The pie chart in Illustration 3.9 can be used to get prospects to agree they are interested in LTC insurance. It is best to review this pie chart after an agent's prospects understand why the perceived payers cover only a small portion of LTC costs.

The agent could say something like: "We have covered a lot of information about long-term care. Let's look at a summary of who pays nursing home care costs. As you can see, about 36 percent of the payments to nursing homes come from ordinary people who pay out of pocket or with insurance. These two methods of payment are lumped together because long-term care insurance benefits are paid directly to the insured, who then pays the facility. Most insurance benefits get credited as out-of-pocket payments. Do you want to use your own money to pay for your care?

"Almost half of nursing home expenses are paid by the joint federal and state means-tested program, Medicaid. We just talked about how difficult it is to qualify for Medicaid benefits. Do you want to virtually bankrupt yourself, then depend on the government to take care of you?

"The result of Medicare's restrictive qualification criteria and limited benefits is that the program pays for just over 12 percent of the total bill. Are you willing to accept these requirements and Medicare's short benefit cycle to pay for your care?

"Charity and some other sources pay for the balance. Do you want to depend on charities or other sources to pay for your care?"

If the prospect answers no to the above questions, the agent has a good prospect for LTC insurance. Now, the agent is ready to move the discussion into a fact-finding interview. Something like the following will provide a transition to fact finding: "Would you like to take a look at an affordable alternative that may make more sense to you than these other options? Before we talk about the products, though, I'd like to get a little more information about you and your thoughts on long-term care." Now the agent is ready to go to the fact-finder. Some agents prefer to complete the fact-finder first. This helps determine how much education about the perceived payers and providers is necessary to convince the prospect to buy the insurance. If the agent has completed the fact-finder already, the transition may go something like this, "Would you like to take a look at an affordable alternative that may make more sense to you than these other options?" If the answer is yes, the agent brings out the product brochure and outline of coverage to discuss the product.

■ SUMMARY

This chapter provides an excellent way to start a discussion with a prospect about LTC insurance. Providing this basic information gives the prospect an understanding of what long-term care means and why some of the perceived payers of LTC are not the best alternatives for most people.

A successful agent takes the time to learn about the need for LTC and the perceived payers. Visiting the local Medicaid application office and a couple of different types of facilities in the area affects dramatically the agent's understanding of the issues underlying LTC. Sharing these personal experiences with prospects can help them learn about LTC issues from someone who has invested the time to become well-informed.

Agents should commit to making those visits. They should practice the system presented in this chapter and meet with clients they currently have relationships with. Agents must help their clients understand the issues surrounding LTC insurance, then find out whether they're interested in talking about the insurance alternative. Using the educational sales method outlined in this chapter will increase the likelihood that prospects will want to learn more about LTC insurance.

■ CHAPTER 3 QUESTIONS FOR REVIEW

1. The average annual cost of nursing home care in 2000 is

   A. $28,000
   B. $38,000
   C. $48,000
   D. $58,000

2. People today are living longer because medical science treats successfully all of the following conditions EXCEPT

   A. diabetes

   B. stroke

   C. heart attack

   D. cancer

3. What are the odds that a 65-year-old will be admitted to a nursing home during his or her lifetime?

   A. 1 out of 5

   B. 2 out of 5

   C. 3 out of 5

   D. 4 out of 5

4. The average stay in a nursing home is how many years?

   A. 2

   B. 2.5

   C. 4

   D. 4.5

5. All of the following statements about Medicare nursing home benefits are true EXCEPT

   A. Medicare is designed to pay for chronic conditions that require nursing home care

   B. care must be provided in a nursing home that is Medicare certified

   C. a doctor must certify that skilled nursing care is required

   D. before entering the nursing home, a patient must have been in a hospital at least three days

4

Fact Finding and Analysis

Many agents begin each meeting with a new prospect by espousing the features and benefits of a particular long-term care insurance policy. They recommend the prospect purchase the same options everyone else has purchased. While these agents may consider this to be selling, it isn't making a suitable sale. A suitable sale matches a prospect's needs to a company's product.

To identify a prospect's insurance needs, an agent must ask the prospect about his or her financial resources and other relevant issues. Asking the right questions is the key to opening the door to the information the agent must have to make the best recommendation for the prospect. Some agents tend to talk at clients, telling them what's good for them. Talking at prospects is a good way to lose their interest. Asking them questions, however, draws them into conversation, and listening carefully to their answers reveals their needs and builds trust.

Some prospects will provide personal information to an agent freely. They discuss openly their personal financial situations, their relationships with their children and even their thoughts on how they want to be cared for as they age. These prospects trust the agent. They know the agent has their best interests at heart and is not just trying to make a sale. Agents must earn this kind of trust every day with every client and prospect. It starts with the initial phone call for an appointment and gains strength throughout the sales and application processes. Referrals to friends and family members show the trust a client has in his or her agent.

Trust is fragile, though. One slip and it can be lost or broken. Each prospect has his or her own level of forgiveness, and agents should not attempt to find out what that level is. Regaining trust is twice as difficult as establishing it.

Some prospects are tight-lipped. They are reluctant to answer an agent's questions and may not do so truthfully. These prospects have not developed the trust necessary to confide their personal situations to the agent. This makes a suitable sale difficult.

Maybe these prospects know what they want to purchase, so they are eager to cut to the chase. Or they may have had a bad experience buying insurance in the past and want the sale to be over quickly. Or perhaps they don't trust insurance agents in general. How can an agent make their purchase of LTC insurance enjoyable? Using this chapter as a general guide to the fact-finding process is the next step in creating a win-win situation.

ILL. 4.1 ■ *A Little Wisdom*

One agent bumped into a brick wall with a couple of clients who used the "We'll go live with our kids" objection. Six months later the agent received a call from the prospects. They had just returned from a weekend with their son, daughter-in-law and three grandchildren. During their visit they realized what a tremendous burden they'd be to their children and grandchildren if they should lose their independence and have to move in with their son for needed care. They decided to purchase LTC insurance as soon as they got home. Time and life frequently reveal the wisdom of an agent's advice and recommendations.

People today want to take some time to think before deciding to purchase a product they will keep many years. Whether they are buying a new car, furniture, pots and pans, or LTC insurance, consumers want to deliberate before committing their hard-earned money. The only place people seem to purchase on impulse anymore is at the grocery store and membership warehouses.

The need to take some time to make a decision is especially true with LTC insurance. It's a new product to most prospects. Their parents didn't own it, and, most likely, their siblings don't own it. Their children don't think they need it. Maybe, just maybe, one or two of their friends have protected themselves with it.

Prospects need time to digest information they have received from agents, insurance companies and any third-party sources they have accessed. They might want to talk the purchasing decision over with their children. They may need to discuss it with their financial advisors, attorneys or accountants. All this takes time.

Those buying LTC insurance today are making a cutting-edge decision. They have shown leadership and obtained the knowledge necessary to make an informed decision based on their personal needs and wants. They can't follow the crowd with a product as new as LTC insurance.

So where does an agent start? What information does he or she need to know? What questions should the agent ask to get needed information?

This chapter offers specific suggestions to help agents obtain the information they need to advise prospects and clients. It addresses what information to ask for, how to ask for it and, most importantly, why it is important to get that information. At the same time, this process helps the agents build trust and make suitable sales.

■ ■ ■ ■ ■

■ FACT FINDING

Agents sell insurance by first gathering facts about prospects—their assets, debts, income and expenses. (Financial planning entails establishing a balance sheet plus

---

ILL. 4.2 ■ *Top Five Reasons People Purchase LTC Insurance*

1. To remain independent and control their own lives and finances, particularly so they won't burden their family, their children especially (25%)

2. Other (25%)—the fact that more than 25% of respondents listed other reasons as the single most important reason indicates that there is a great deal of diversity in purchase motivation

3. To protect their assets from being spent on LTC services (23%)

4. To protect their standard of living (15%)

5. To pay for LTC services when needed (12%)

---

a budget or an income statement.) Once these facts are known, the agents can make suitable recommendations.

A key element of fact finding that has disappeared gradually over the years is gathering information about how clients feel about something. A suitable long-term care insurance sale must include feeling finding as part of fact finding.

Feeling-finding questions explore how prospects feel about various issues. How do they want to be cared for as they age? Do they want their spouses or children to take active roles in providing care? Do they want to pay for a portion of their own care out of excess income? Do they want to be cared for at home? What do they want to happen when they no longer can be cared for at home? Do they feel the government owes them something for all the years they paid taxes?

Financial facts are relatively easy to obtain compared to information about how prospects feel about health-related issues. Most prospects haven't taken the time to think about these questions, and agents need their answers to analyze the prospects' LTC situations. Without this information, an agent could make a poor recommendation.

Poor recommendations can lead to undesirable results. The most obvious occurs when no application is taken because an agent and a consumer have not achieved a meeting of the minds. Another possible result occurs when an application is taken and the policy is issued, but the applicant doesn't accept the policy. Some people think the applicant got cold feet. Actually, the applicant's policy refusal indicates that not enough information was shared and that the prospect and agent did not have a clear understanding of each other's feelings. A third possible result occurs when a client lapses his or her policy soon after it's issued. A final poor result occurs when the policy is replaced by another agent who is able to obtain better information.

The fact-finding process seems laborious to some agents. These agents are anxious to sell. Asking a bunch of questions takes too much energy for them. However, the time spent trying to understand a prospect's situation pays dividends in the long run.

Taking the time to understand the client's circumstances and to identify his or her needs and wishes builds trust between the agent and the prospect, and the information obtained results in a better recommendation. Such an approach to agent-client relationships also facilitates compliance with market conduct rules and regulations.

In today's litigious society, many professionals have found themselves subject to second-guessing by people who expect nothing less than perfection from advisors. Whether it is a doctor's diagnosis, an accountant's interpretation of tax laws or an insurance agent's advice, everyone is under careful scrutiny these days. Performing a thorough assessment of a prospect's personal situation, then maintaining that fact-finder in the client's file, can prove invaluable should an agent's recommendations ever be questioned.

■ THE FACT-FINDING FORM

Agents enjoy many advantages in keeping all client information assembled in one central location —a fact-finding form. This tool is an essential component of a suitable sale. Completing the form helps agents to:

- develop trust with the prospect;

- organize the initial meeting;

- obtain valuable information for future use; and

- document the fact-finding conversation.

Each agent must make a diligent effort to obtain the information the fact-finding form requires. Some prospects will provide all the information freely while others will not. The reluctant prospect either doesn't trust the agent or doesn't understand why the agent needs the information. Trust develops over time. The agent can explain why he or she needs the information as the agent asks the questions.

It's important to ask questions that are relevant and useful. For example, asking about a prospect's hobbies and finding out one of them is golf is important for the underwriting process. Asking how much a prospect paid for his or her country club membership is not relevant and may seem too personal to the prospect, thus hindering the development of trust.

The following fact-finder was developed to help agents understand the range of information needed to make a suitable sale. As with all fact-finders, it should be reviewed and approved by the compliance department of an agent's insurance company. The questions on the sample form in Illustration 4.3 all have a purpose, which is explained in the annotations that follow the form. Take a few minutes before reading the annotations to familiarize yourself with the questions in the fact finder. Complete one using information on yourself to better understand the flow.

ILL. 4.3 ▪ *Blank Fact-Finder Form*

① **Name:**_____   ② **Spouse's Name:**_____

Birthdate:_____   **Birthdate:**_____

③ **Home Street Address:**_____

City/State/Zip:_____

④ **Home Phone:**_____   **Business Phone (W):**_____

Mobile Phone:_____   **Fax:**_____

E-Mail Address:_____

⑤ **CHILDREN**

Name	Age	Lives In
_____	_____	_____
_____	_____	_____
_____	_____	_____
_____	_____	_____
_____	_____	_____

⑥ Do any of your children have any special needs?

_____

_____

⑦ Tell me about your hobbies.

_____

_____

⑧ Tell me about your career.

_____

_____

⑨ Why did you decide to retire? - OR- Why did you decide to continue working?

_____

_____

ILL. 4.3 ■ *Blank Fact-Finder Form (cont.)*

⑩ What are your current sources of income?

_____

_____

INCOME

Wages, Salary, etc.	$ _____	Social Security	$ _____
Pension Income	$ _____	401(K) Income	$ _____
Annuity Income	$ _____	Investment Income	$ _____
Trust Income	$ _____	Other Sources	$ _____

Total Income $ _____

⑪ Do you plan to retire in your current home?

_____

_____

⑫ What types of insurance do you maintain? Do you normally purchase a low or high deductible?

_____

_____

⑬ Is your Medicare-supplement plan covering all the items you expected?

_____

_____

⑭ **LIVING EXPENSES**

Mortgage/Rent	$ _____	Utilities	$ _____
Food	$ _____	Entertainment	$ _____
Insurance	$ _____	Transportation	$ _____
Vacations	$ _____	Medical Expenses	$ _____
Taxes	$ _____	Debts	$ _____
Charities & Church	$ _____	Other Expenses	$ _____

Total Living Expenses $ _____

Total Income Less Total Expenses $ _____

⑮ Where have you been able to save or invest the most successfully?

_____

_____

⑯ How well have you been able to diversify your retirement nest egg?

_____

_____

ILL. 4.3 ■ *Blank Fact-Finder Form (cont.)*

⑰ Are some of your assets in tax-deferred or tax-exempt vehicles?

_____

_____

⑱ **SAVINGS AND INVESTMENTS**

Checking Accounts	$ _____	Savings Accounts	$ _____
Certificates of Deposit	$ _____	Mutual Funds	$ _____
Life Ins. Cash Values	$ _____	Annuities	$ _____
Stocks	$ _____	Bonds	$ _____
Real Estate	$ _____	401(K)	$ _____
IRAs	$ _____	Pensions	$ _____
Other Liquid Assets	$ _____		

Total Savings and Investments $ _____

PROPERTY

Principal Residence	$ _____	Other Homes	$ _____
Investment Property	$ _____	Personal Property	$ _____
Valuables	$ _____	Vehicles	$ _____
Recreational Vehicles	$ _____	Business Interests	$ _____
Other Property	$ _____		

Total Property $ _____

Total Assets $ _____

⑲ Have you been able to pay off some of your debts?

_____

_____

⑳ What debts do you have outstanding?

_____

_____

LIABILITIES

Principle Mortgage	$ _____	Home Equity Loan	$ _____
Credit Cards	$ _____	Installment Loans	$ _____
Other Debts	$ _____		

Total Liabilities $ _____

Net Worth   **(assets minus liabilities)** $ _____

ILL. 4.3 ■ *Blank Fact-Finder Form (cont.)*

(21) What types of legal planning have you done regarding your death or a possible illness?

_____

_____

Trusts?	Yes / No	Will?	Yes / No
Living Will?	Yes / No	Power of Attorney?	Yes / No
Durable Power of Attorney?	Yes / No	Other _____	

(22) **ADVISORS**   Name   Location

Attorney   _____   _____

Accountant   _____   _____

Banker\Trust Officer _____   _____

Insurance Agent   _____   _____

Other Advisor   _____   _____

(23) What experience have you had with someone needing long-term care?

_____

_____

(24) What circumstances required them to need the care?

_____

_____

(25) As you become old, how do you want to be cared for?

_____

_____

(26) Under what circumstances would you have to enter a nursing home as you age?

_____

_____

(27) What do you know about the cost of care in the area?

_____

_____

(28) If you had to enter a nursing home today, how would you pay for your care?

_____

_____

■ ANNOTATED FACT-FINDING QUESTIONS

As mentioned earlier, the questions on the sample form all have a purpose. The following annotations will clarify that purpose as they guide the agent through the questions.

1. Name and birthdate

The agent needs the prospect's birthday to determine the prospect's age. Requesting a birthdate is easier than asking, "How old are you?" It is also helpful for those insurance companies that use the nearest birthday rather than actual age. The agent can use the date of birth in completing the application and add the prospect's name to the agent's birthday card list. Some agents like to get this information when they schedule an appointment.

2. Spouse's name and birthdate

Asking for the spouse's name can be a bit sensitive if a divorce, separation, death or similar event has occurred. It is easier to get the information over the phone when making the appointment or to take a clue from the prospect's ring finger when deciding whether to ask about a spouse. If the spouse has died, the survivor may be willing to discuss the circumstances. The prospect may have been a caregiver and "may never want to go through that again," as many ex-caregivers say.

3. Address

This is necessary information for various reasons, including meetings and mailings.

4. Contact Information

The important question to be answered here is what forms of communication the prospect prefers. Getting all of the phone numbers and e-mail addresses is of secondary importance. People older than age 60 are the fastest growing segment of Internet users. Many use e-mail to communicate with children and grandchildren, especially when distance prevents them from seeing one another.

5. Children

The agent has several good reasons for raising this topic:

– An LTC policyowner's children are the people most likely to file a claim. For this reason, an agent needs their names and addresses.

– The agent can use this question as an opportunity to prepare to overcome the "my kids will take care of me" objection. For example, if the children live on one coast and the client lives in the Midwest, it is geographically impossible for the children to care for the parents.

– The agent can use the information to suggest that if the children are raising their own families, they may be unwilling or unable to care for their parents, too.

– The children also are prospects for LTC insurance.

– When completing an application, many insurance companies ask whether the applicant wants a third party notified in the event the policy is about to lapse because of nonpayment of premiums. A trusted, responsible child is a perfect person to receive such notification.

6. Do any of your children have any special needs?

This question is used to determine whether:

– the prospect has had caregiving responsibilities for a long period of time in raising his or her own children;

– any of the children are ruled out as caregivers;

– the prospect still provides care to an adult child (if so, the agent should learn of any plans to care for this child after the prospect's death or disability); and

– the prospect's home is considered exempt for Medicaid purposes because a disabled or dependent child lives there.

7. Tell me about your hobbies.

This question helps the agent identify the prospect's interests and activities, including volunteer activities, which is useful information for underwriting purposes. It also enables the agent to identify common interests, which may enhance the trust between the prospect and the agent.

8. Tell me about your career.

Asking the question this way encourages the prospect to talk about his or her accomplishments. The information gives the agent valuable insight into what the prospect considers important. Listening to this story alone forges considerable trust between the agent and the prospect.

9. Why did you decide to retire? -OR- Why did you decide to continue working?

The agent should use information gained from the previous query to determine which of these two questions to ask. Some people have had to retire for health reasons, which is a cause for concern when underwriting an application. Some retired because they were ready to, while others retired because they were downsized or received early retirement packages. Maybe the prospect is looking for a second career.

On the other hand, some people continue to work because they need the money, which is a cause for concern when determining the type of policy that will meet a prospect's budget. A younger prospect still working is normal. Others just like going to work. They think they still have much to contribute and they like the peer interaction. Some get part-time jobs they think of as hobbies. These people feel like they get paid to do something they love to do.

10. What are your current sources of income?

This question is an easy way to open a discussion about finances. If trust has been developed properly, the prospect will share this information. Getting information here makes getting the more detailed data below easier. Many additional reasons for delving into current sources of income include the following:

- The agent uses this information to develop the prospect's income statement. Some prospects appreciate receiving complete analyses of their financial situations. However, getting the exact dollar amount for each of the listed items is less important than discovering a prospect's source of funds.

- The information can be used to identify a payment source for the LTC premiums.

- Obtaining a total income figure is very important when completing the suitability worksheet many insurance companies require.

- Some people think individuals should not spend more than a certain percentage of their incomes on LTC insurance. Each prospect must decide how much he or she is willing to pay for the peace of mind that accompanies LTC coverage. No single percentage of income is perfect for all people. Each person values his or her purchases differently, which is why so many different cars, homes and even toasters and vacuum cleaners are available. An expenditure that is extravagant to one person is prudent to another.

- An agent executing a suitable sale makes recommendations, then leaves it up to the prospect to determine how much he or she wants to spend on LTC insurance. No general rules exist.

11. Do you plan to retire in your current home?

The answer to this question tells the agent whether home care is important to the prospect. If the prospect's home is his or her castle, the prospect will prefer to receive care there. If the prospect is not attached to his or her home, moving to a facility will not have the emotional impact it does for many people. Often, people simplify their life-styles in retirement by moving into condominiums, smaller homes, or ranch-style homes with no stairs. Asking this question also gives an indication of the prospect's intent to:

- move to a warmer climate;

- move closer to his or her children or grandchildren;

    – purchase a retirement or vacation home; or

    – move to a continuing care retirement community (CCRC).

The prospect may be concerned about the cost of care where he or she plans to retire. Having this information makes servicing the prospect easier. If the prospect plans to move, the agent can put him or her in touch with a person from the agent's company or someone the agent knows from industry activity in the new area.

Asking this question here leads into the rent or mortgage amount in the list of expense items below. Some agents prefer to ask this question when they discuss the value of the home in the fact-finder's property section.

12. What types of insurance do you maintain? Do you normally purchase a low or high deductible?

The answer to this question tells the agent a lot about his or her chances of selling an LTC policy. If the prospect owns only homeowner's and auto insurance, he or she may resist purchasing LTC insurance. If the prospect owns life, disability income, Medicare-supplement and other forms of insurance, the prospect obviously appreciates the peace of mind owning insurance brings. This information also is used in completing the list of expenses below. Some agents like to itemize all insurance the prospect pays for while others like to lump it in one sum. The list of expenses here offers a single line item for all insurance expenses combined. The second part of the question about deductibles is helpful information to have when deciding which elimination period to recommend. This is discussed in more detail in the next chapter.

13. Is your Medicare-supplement plan covering all the items you expected?

If the agent sells Medicare-supplement insurance, this question is a good way to open a conversation about that type of coverage. If the prospect doesn't like his or her current coverage, it may be an opportunity for the agent to sell a more comprehensive plan. If the prospect pays for benefits he or she no longer needs, reducing the coverage may be in order. Other reasons for asking this question follow:

    – The agent gains an insight into the prospect's risk tolerance. For example, if the prospect doesn't own any Medicare-supplement coverage, he or she is willing to accept more risk. If the prospect owns one of the more comprehensive plans, he or she is risk adverse and may give serious consideration to a complete LTC insurance plan.

    – The question also provides an opportunity to discuss Medicare and the prospect's feelings about that program. Those with a thorough understanding of Medicare know it imposes many requirements to qualify for benefits, requires many deductibles and copayments and offers limited benefits. These prospects also may understand how Medicare's at-home recovery and skilled nursing facility benefits work. Such prospects most likely will appreciate why purchasing LTC insurance fills a void left by government programs.

14. What are your current living expenses?

The prospect's answers to the following questions reveal where the prospect spends his or her income. Obtaining an exact figure for each item is of secondary importance to helping the prospect understand where he or she spends money. If the agent performs a financial analysis for the prospect, exact information is essential. Without this information about the prospect's expenses, only half of the financial analysis is completed. Answers to the questions also are helpful in finding premium dollars for LTC insurance. The prospect may not realize how much he or she spends on an item that actually is not a priority for the prospect.

The agent should remember the following when asking about itemized living expenses:

- Insurance—The agent should include all insurance premiums, including the Medicare Part B premium.

- Taxes—This includes income, sales, personal property and real estate property taxes. The amounts and percentages vary by state. The agent should find out whether the prospect itemizes his or her deductions. If so, and if the unreimbursed medical expenses shown above are average, the prospect may find the tax deductibility of a tax-qualified LTC plan beneficial.

- Medical expenses—This includes unreimbursed medical expenses, such as prescription medications, eyeglasses, physical examinations and dental care. The total amount varies depending on the type of medical insurance the prospect has at work, the Medicare plan chosen and the Medicare-supplement insurance owned. The answer can lead to a general discussion about the prospect's current health condition and his or her health history. The information is important for underwriting considerations. The agent shouldn't be alarmed when he or she realizes the prospect has extensive unreimbursed medical expenses. AARP estimates the average senior spends 19 percent of his or her income on such expenses—many times for items that will not disqualify a prospect from LTC insurance.

A positive figure on the line for *total income less total expenses* indicates the excess income the prospect has to pay LTC insurance premiums. A suitable sale is made when some income remains after adding the cost of LTC insurance premiums. A suitable sale cannot be made if the prospect's expenses exceed his or her income. In this case, the insurance is clearly unaffordable for the prospect. In some situations, however, one of the prospect's children pays the LTC insurance premiums, especially when the child lives far away and is relatively affluent. Getting more than one child to pay the premium is a difficult challenge. The agent first must get them to agree it is the right thing to do, then must convince them to make the payments. Children paying for or subsidizing the premiums makes it a suitable sale regardless of the prospect's financial situation.

15. Where have you been able to save or invest the most successfully?

This question is key to finding out whether the prospect has assets to protect by purchasing LTC insurance. Many prospects like to talk about their investments—especially the good ones.

16. How well have you been able to diversify your retirement nest egg?

The answer to this question, too, tells the agent whether the prospect has assets that need to be protected by LTC insurance. It also is important for the following reasons:

– It provides information about the prospect's risk tolerance. For example, prospects who invest in common stocks are likely to accept more risks than prospects who invest in bonds and mutual funds. Prospects who invest only in bank certificates of deposit probably don't want to accept much risk. Such knowledge of a prospect's risk tolerance is invaluable in designing an LTC plan that meets his or her needs and wants.

– In asking this question, the agent also may discover that the prospect has not found someone the prospect can trust to manage his or her retirement nest egg. If the agent is licensed to sell investments, he or she can help the prospect diversify or simplify the prospect's portfolio.

17. Are some of your assets in tax-deferred or tax-exempt vehicles?

Most people invest their retirement funds in these types of vehicles, so the question often starts a conversation about taxes, tax-advantaged investing and investment options. The agent can use the information from this discussion to decide what type of LTC insurance plan to recommend. For example, if a prospect has not taken advantage of available tax breaks, it may mean that tax matters don't influence his or her decisions. Consequently, in making a presentation to such a prospect, an agent may focus on the difference between various benefit triggers in a policy rather than on the tax benefits of the particular plan. On the other hand, if a prospect has invested a large portion of his or her retirement dollars in tax-advantaged vehicles, an agent would recommend and emphasize the tax advantages of a tax-qualified policy.

Some prospects may be unaware of the advantages of putting funds in an annuity to pay for LTC premiums. Agents should discuss this topic with their prospects because many times a prospect finds that putting a portion of his or her savings into a single-premium immediate annuity, then using those proceeds to pay the LTC insurance premiums is an excellent alternative to writing a check each time a premium is due. While such sales often sound great to both prospects and agents, some risks are involved. An agent must fully disclose all relevant facts. For example, the agent must explain that while the income from the annuity is guaranteed for life, the LTC insurance premiums can be adjusted in the future.

18. Savings and Investments

The information asked for in this section of the fact-finder is an essential component of the prospect's assets. If the agent is undertaking a full analysis of the prospect's financial situation, a balance sheet must be completed. The balance sheet lists both assets and liabilities to determine net worth. Savings and investments are considered liquid assets—that is, assets that can be converted into cash quickly. If the prospect is not interested in a complete financial analysis, obtaining approximate figures in this section helps the agent determine what liquid assets the prospect may be interested in protecting. The securities-licensed agent may find opportunities to move some dollars from one area to another when current allocations are not meeting the prospect's long-term saving objectives.

The following should be noted about these items under savings and investments:

- Life insurance cash values—Some companies let clients use life insurance cash values or dividends to pay LTC premiums. As long as this payment source does not diminish the purpose of a prospect's life insurance program, it is a good alternative. The option requires careful analysis when the life insurance proceeds are "spent" already. This occurs, for example, in an estate plan in which the life insurance is designed to pay the estate taxes or in a pension maximization plan in which the proceeds will become an income stream for the surviving spouse.

- Real estate—This line is for investments in real estate investment trusts (REITs), partnerships or other real estate that can be sold quickly and converted into cash. Investment and rental properties fit better with the fixed assets listed under property, below.

- Annuities—Some insurance companies' computer systems allow clients to pay LTC premiums with annuity proceeds. This is a good alternative to writing a check every year. Clients must understand, however, that while annuity income is guaranteed for life, the long-term care premium is adjustable.

- 401(K)—These amounts may be accounted for on other lines. Some prospects think of their 401(K) plans and IRAs as separate investments. Others like to combine them as a single investment. In any event, the agent should make sure not to count these amounts twice.

The following should be noted about these items under property:

- Principal residence—Many people believe their homes never can be taken away. For Medicaid purposes, a principal residence is considered an exempt asset only when:

  - the nursing home resident is expected to return home within six months;

  - a spouse of the resident continues to live in the home;

- a disabled child lives in the home;

- a sibling with an ownership interest has lived there for at least a year; or

- a child has lived in the home for at least two years and taken care of the parent now living in the nursing home.

— Investment property—This likely is counted twice for Medicaid qualification purposes—once as an asset, then again as the revenue generated is considered income for Medicaid purposes.

— Valuables—Each nursing home resident on Medicaid can keep one engagement ring and one wedding ring. Other valuables are considered countable assets.

— Other homes—Vacation or summer homes must be sold to qualify for Medicaid.

— Personal property—Items of personal property are exempt assets for Medicaid qualification purposes.

— Vehicles—A vehicle is exempt from Medicaid if it is:

- worth less than a certain amount ($4,500 in many states);

- used to drive to work or medical appointments; or

- adapted for a handicapped person.

— Total assets—This final amount is considered for Medicaid qualification, as discussed in detail in Chapter 3. Briefly, Medicaid exempts:

- the home as long as a spouse, disabled child or sibling with an ownership interest in the home lives in it;

- personal property;

- wedding rings; and

- a car as long as the nursing home resident or spouse continues to use it.

If the prospect is already at or near the poverty level, LTC insurance is not suitable for him or her. Some advisors say LTC insurance isn't appropriate for someone who has just $50,000 or a couple with just $100,000 or even $250,000. These people think the prospects are so close to spending down to Medicaid levels they might just as well throw in the towel, not worry about how to finance their care and become wards of the state.

What the advisors fail to realize is that LTC insurance is designed to protect people's pride and dignity—not just their financial resources. Someone's pride and dignity can be as securely bound to his or her independence as to that person's assets. Independent people don't want to burden their children with their care, and they want to choose the locations and the types of facilities in which they receive care.

19. Have you been able to pay off some of your debts?

Most retired people have reduced their debts, and they're not interested in adding more. Many are proud of the fact that they're debt free and own their homes. Debts, including mortgages, are not considered for Medicaid qualification.

20. What debts do you have outstanding?

This leads directly into a discussion of the liabilities listed below. The agent should keep in mind that liabilities do not affect Medicaid qualification. Furthermore, the prospect must maintain a certain level of income to continue making payments on the debt.

The information on liabilities is needed to complete a thorough financial analysis and to arrive at a net worth figure. The agent should remember the following about these items:

– Credit cards—The agent should include nothing if the prospect pays off the balances each month.

– Installment loans—This includes automobile loans, business loans and any other loan from a bank or another lending institution.

– Other debts—This includes amounts owed to friends and family members.

This net worth (assets minus liabilities) is the amount of money the prospect has at risk. Although Medicaid doesn't consider actual net worth, most prospects think of this as the amount they could lose.

21. What types of legal planning have you done regarding your death or a possible illness?

The answer to this question gives the agent an understanding of the issues important to the prospect and what the prospect has done to address those issues. Any Medicaid estate planning the prospect has done will be revealed now.

The agent should remember the following about the itemized list:

– Trusts—Sometimes a prospect with a high net worth shifts assets into an irrevocable trust to qualify for Medicaid. Such a trust must be established and assets placed in it at least 60 months before applying for Medicaid. If not, the Medicaid applicant goes through a period of incligibility that can last varying lengths of time depending on the amount transferred and the cost of care in the state.

For someone who has successfully established a trust to avoid spending all of his or her assets before qualifying for Medicaid, the state's estate recovery program looms over the trust. Each state has a right to recover from the trust or other means an amount equal to the amount the state paid for the Medicaid recipient's care. The nice thing about trusts from the state's point of view is that a complete accounting of all amounts and beneficiaries is documented. The state knows where to go to recover assets.

– Living will—Many people have set up living wills to make the Medicaid qualification process easier. What they don't realize is that to make the Medicaid qualification process easier, money must be transferred with no strings attached; that is, it must be an irrevocable transfer. By definition, a living will is revocable and the assets placed in one do not qualify as exempt or unattainable; therefore, they are counted for Medicaid qualification.

– Durable power of attorney—This is an agreement that if a condition arises because of which a person is incapable of making decisions, someone else will make the decisions for the person. Durable powers of attorney are essential for claimants entering claim status because of cognitive impairments. LTC benefits cannot be paid directly to people with cognitive impairments—either durable powers of attorney or guardianships must be established.

– Will—Making a will is the minimum amount of planning a person should complete before a crisis occurs.

– Power of attorney—If a power of attorney is established because of which the prospect is incapable of making decisions on his or her own, two concerns arise. The first, a legal concern, is whether such a prospect is able to enter into an agreement, such as the agreement involved in purchasing insurance. Second, is the prospect insurable? This is a risk management/underwriting and suitability concern. Did the prospect have to sign a power of attorney because of a cognitive impairment?

– Other—People use many other methods in planning for death or disability. Having the prospect's plan documented is helpful. If it is a method unknown to the agent, a call to the prospect's advisor is appropriate.

22. Advisors

Knowing who advises the prospect is important for the following reasons:

– It positions the agent as the professional the prospect uses for LTC insurance advice.

– It provides a name for the third-party notification of lapse on the LTC insurance application.

– It documents others who should be contacted in the event of a claim.

– It provides the agent with a resource he or she can use to refer clients with similar needs.

– It helps the agent develop new centers of influence.

The agent should note the following about each prospective advisor:

– Attorney—People frequently consult their attorneys on LTC issues. Some advocates recommend such consultation before purchasing LTC insurance policies.

– Accountant—The prospect is encouraged to seek advice from his or her accountant or tax advisor to determine the benefits of owning a tax-qualified or nontax-qualified LTC insurance policy. The agent should know this person in the event the advisor is unfamiliar with the subject. The agent need not tell the accountant what advice to give, but rather explain which tax forms a claimant must complete. Each claimant receives Form 1099-LTC from the insurance company and is instructed to complete Form 8853, which explains how to account for benefits received from a tax-qualified LTC insurance policy. The agent should have a copy of these forms and the instructions for completing Form 8853. Appendix C contains the 1999 version.

– Banker/trust officer—If the prospect has established a trust to qualify for Medicaid, the agent might want to confirm it is an irrevocable trust and when it was established. As far as Medicaid is concerned, a Medicaid applicant owns any assets put in a trust within 60 months before entering a nursing home. Some prospects find it valuable to own LTC insurance during this five-year period to ensure that they don't have to liquidate assets to pay for their care. Knowing whom to call to get the details is important. The agent also may wish to contact the prospect's attorney who drafted the trust documents, but he or she may not know when the assets were placed in the trust.

– Insurance agent—The prospect may list many agents, including those from whom he or she purchased homeowner's, automobile, life, disability income and other insurance policies. This also discloses to the agent any relationships or loyalties that might interfere with the prospect's willingness to do business with the agent.

– Other advisors—This is a good open-ended question to ask all prospects. Some people like to get their financial advice from their Uncle Vinny, a neighbor or golf partner, magazines or some other free source. In many cases, a prospect gets what he or she pays for—unless, of course, the source referred the prospect to the agent.

■ ANNOTATED FEELING-FINDING QUESTIONS

An agent can ask many feeling-finding questions. The best ones pull a prospect into a conversation about long-term care—and not just LTC insurance. Overwhelming prospects with dramatic statistics about nursing home use usually pushes them away from meaningful dialogue.

Before asking prospects the questions below, an agent should answer them with himself or herself. If married, the agent's spouse should answer the same questions.

ILL. 4.4 ■ *A Little Wisdom*

You can lead a horse to water, but you can't make it drink. The same is true of prospects for LTC insurance. You can lead them to the product, but you can't make them buy it. How do successful LTC agents get prospects to buy? First, an agent interests the prospect in the need for the product by asking questions and listening to the answers. The prospect becomes engaged in the conversation and interested in the coverage. When the prospect agrees that a need for LTC insurance exists and wants to talk about it, the agent begins educating the client about the product. The successful agent makes prospects so thirsty for LTC insurance that they want to have it.

This exercise reinforces the agent's personal beliefs about LTC insurance and gives the agent considerable empathy when prospects struggle to answer the more provocative questions.

Although the following questions conclude the fact-finder, *some agents prefer to ask a prospect these questions at the beginning of the discussion about LTC.* They are designed to make the prospect thirsty, so to speak. Knowing the answers helps both the prospect and the agent understand one another better.

23. **What experience have you had with someone needing long-term care?**

People with personal experiences with long-term care are more receptive to discussing the subject. If a person has been a caregiver, for example, the experience probably had a major effect on his or her life. If a loved one needed professional LTC assistance recently, the prospect knows the high cost of providing this type of care. Personal experience helps prospects understand how stressful LTC situations are. Caregiving is physically, emotionally and financially draining. Frequently, these three types of stress compound and create exhaustion, which often motivates the primary caregiver to seek help. LTC insurance provides the money to cover the cost of assistance. Paying a little bit for insurance rather than a lot when the need for long-term care arises is a prudent decision for most prospects.

This feeling-finding question starts to uncover prospects' sources of pride and dignity, which may have financial, emotional or physical roots. If prospects have personal experience with LTC, they'll know how easily people can lose their pride and dignity—especially when they must depend on the government to pay for their care.

24. **What circumstances required that person to need the care?**

This question leads prospects to paint pictures of conditions that have resulted in others needing care. If they can picture needing care themselves or even someone else needing care, they become better prospects.

ILL. 4.5 ■ *A Little Wisdom*

An 'old man' sat in the back of the room during a long-term care seminar. when the seminar ended, he approached the speaker and said, "I don't think this is the right type of insurance for me. I'm only 86 years old. But I have brother who is 93, so I'll mention it to him." Remember: old is state of mind, not of age!

A prospect's source of pride and dignity may reside in maintaining independence and not burdening others. Asking this question helps the prospect realize that if it happened to a friend or family member, it could happen to the prospect some day.

Many prospects already have answered this question by answering the first. Requesting more details about what caused their loved ones to need care supports and advances the picture-painting process. An agent may want to ask questions to confirm what he or she already has been told: "Did you say it was cancer that caused your brother to need care? Where did the cancer start? How long did he need care? Did he recover?"

A good rhetorical follow-up question to ask after listening to the answers to these questions is: "It could happen to any of us, couldn't it?"

25. As you become old, how do you want to be cared for?

No one considers himself or herself old, but everyone wants to live to an old age. Research has found that most people older than age 50 think an old person is about 15 years older than they are. Using the phrase *as you become old* recognizes this and asks the prospect to look into the future. Stating the question this way helps the prospect visualize living a long time—until he or she is old.

Good long-term care prospects are still physically independent. They do not want to be taken care of today, but recognize they may need some assistance as they *become old*. What do they want to have happen? Whom do they want to help? Whom do they expect to help them? Again, questions asking for more details help prospects create vivid pictures for themselves, which they then share with their agents in answering the questions.

The answer to this question provides insight into the amount of pride and dignity a prospect possesses. Little pride and dignity exists if the prospect expresses no concern about his or her care. From a suitability standpoint, the answer gives the agent direction on whether home care insurance is appropriate.

26. **Under what circumstances would you have to enter a nursing home as you age?**

This question changes the picture-painting process from general to specific. Answering the query helps the prospect picture an event or a condition that would result in the prospect needing care in the future. The prospect's answer gives the agent insight into what would have to happen for the prospect to collect on his or her long-term care insurance policy.

The answer may be realistic (such as, "If I had a stroke") or it may be unrealistic (such as, "If I'm in an auto accident in which my wife is killed and I'm paralyzed"). Whatever answer is given, it helps the prospect see it happening to him or her someday.

Sources of pride and dignity are evident here. For example, if a prospect's home truly is his or her castle, the prospect will not leave it unless something unusual happens. If the prospect places high value on his or her assets, the prospect might go to a nursing home only after everything is liquidated.

Prospects' true feelings about themselves and their families come out when they answer this question. Some people would rather die than go to a nursing home. The home care benefits of an LTC insurance policy will appeal to these people. A wife may realize how difficult it would be to care for her overweight husband if his health worsened. Having him in a facility so she could provide less physical and more emotional support might make sense to the couple.

The answer to this question also provides an excellent opportunity to explain how someone would qualify for benefits under an LTC policy. An agent should recognize that the prospect probably is thinking of medical problems, while most policies trigger benefits when a physical or cognitive impairment exists.The following is a good way to make the transition:

"Normally after a stroke, people are unable to do things we normally take for granted, such as taking a bath, getting dressed or moving from a bed to a chair. Others may suffer a loss in their ability to remember things or in their orientation to people or time. These types of deficiencies trigger benefits in this type of LTC policy. The insurance company assesses what it calls your *activities of daily living (ADLs)* and your cognitive abilities. Specifically, it considers someone impaired when he or she is unable to perform at least two ADLs." The agent should continue with how the prospect would qualify for benefits under the policy being represented.

27. **What do you know about the cost of care in the area?**

This question is asked for two reasons:

– The prospect may be looking for an insurance company to pay his or her long-term care bill—the prospect is familiar with LTC costs because the prospect needs care and doesn't want to pay his or her own way at a nursing home.

— The prospect may be unaware of the increases in the cost of care that have occurred recently. If the prospect's grandmother needed care 30 years ago, it probably was somewhat more affordable back then. Today, few people can manage a bill for $48,000 or more a year.

The agent should not ask this question unless he or she knows the answer. If neither the agent nor the prospect is aware of the local costs, any trust developed so far based on knowledge will vanish. Without knowing these costs, it is too difficult to establish a need for the product, then design a suitable policy to meet that need.

The more an agent knows about the local providers and their costs the better. Agents should call various providers of care, including nursing homes, assisted living facilities, home care providers, and adult day care centers, to survey the local market. They should get an understanding of the services the caregivers provide, their specialties and payment mechanisms.

Better yet, agents should visit some providers of LTC services and spend time discussing their challenges and opportunities. The agents can ask them about Medicare and Medicaid, about their competition and about how they think the LTC provider network will evolve. Because providers work with people who need care, they recognize what happens as people age and may turn out to be good LTC insurance prospects and centers of influence.

While they visit LTC facilities, agents should take the opportunity to visit some of the residents and ask them about their careers, their families and why they live in the facilities. The agents also benefit by having new real-life stories about people they know to share with prospects so the prospects can better understand the challenge in planning for their LTC needs.

28. **If you had to enter a nursing home today, how would you pay for your care?**

This question helps the agent understand the prospect's primary objection to the insurance option: what alternatives the prospect has, or thinks he or she has, to pay nursing home bills. Some think the government pays for their care. Some have small nest eggs set aside to pay the bills. Some think they can pay for care out of their income. The vast majority of prospects have no idea how they would pay for care.

Prospects who think the government will pay for their long-term care must be made to understand how difficult it is to qualify for Medicare reimbursement of LTC costs, as well as the limited nature of Medicare's LTC benefits. Agents also must understand how the Medicaid program functions at the federal, state and local levels, and they must be able to explain the program to prospects. However, the level of detail to give prospects varies, depending on the prospects' interests and curiosity. Once prospects understand these programs, it's likely they won't want to rely on them to meet their LTC needs.

If a prospect plans to sell assets, the agent learns which of the prospect's assets has the least value to the prospect because it will be the one he or she sells first to cover the nursing home bill. An alternative for the prospect to consider is to transform the asset into an income-producing vehicle, such as an annuity or a mutual fund, and use the interest to pay LTC premiums.

Those expecting to pay for care from income are in for a surprise. Most prospects' pension incomes do not increase, while inflation makes it more and more difficult to purchase needed goods and services as they age. To pay for services with excess income, a prospect must have a stellar performing investment portfolio or be extremely wealthy in the first place.

If the cost of long-term care continues to accelerate at current levels, it will double every 15 years. Paying for this ever-increasing expense can devastate a modest retirement nest egg, significantly reduce a sizable one and deplete most others. Many well-to-do couples have purchased LTC insurance to shift the risk from their estates to insurance companies. These people can afford the LTC premiums easily.

From a suitability standpoint, it is important to know what each prospect thinks is a valid source of funds to pay for long-term care. The prospects with 20-20 hindsight could claim that their agents did not assess thoroughly the prospects' understanding of long-term care, and, therefore, were negligent in providing the information the prospects needed to make informed decisions. Asking this question divulges a prospect's preconceived notion of where the money will come from and helps identify what additional information the prospect will find helpful in making a good decision about the insurance option. It doesn't hurt to ask the same question later in the sales process, after explaining why the prospect's perceived payer of long-term care is not a good alternative.

■ SUMMARY

People point to the demographic shift in America as representing untapped potential for long-term care insurance. There is no denying this. But demographics don't buy insurance—individuals do. An agent is responsible for assessing a prospect's need for the coverage and ability to pay the premiums. This fact-finder helps with both.

The fact-finding process focuses on an individual, not a theoretical member of a demographic group. The process of completing the fact-finder includes many opportunities to discuss personal and financial issues with the prospect. Asking the right questions and listening carefully to the prospect's answers, then responding appropriately and in a concerned and caring manner can forge a bond of trust between the agent and the prospect that has the power to turn the prospect into a devoted client for life.

Practical application of the fact-finder is found in Chapter 7, "Case Studies in Long-Term Care Suitability." The case studies show how to analyze these fact-finding and feeling-finding questions to make an initial recommendation for coverage.

■ CHAPTER 4 QUESTIONS FOR REVIEW

1. All of the following are benefits of the fact-finding process EXCEPT

   A. it builds trust between the agent and the prospect

   B. it results in a better recommendation

   C. it reduces the annual premium

   D. it facilitates compliance with market conduct rules and regulations

2. Which of the following is the key to opening the door to the information an agent needs to make the best recommendation for a client?

   A. Obtaining inspection and credit reports

   B. Asking the right questions

   C. Visiting the client in his or her home or at work

   D. Completing a family medical history

3. Which of the following questions gives an agent direction on whether home care insurance is appropriate?

   A. "As you become old, how do you want to be cared for?"

   B. "What experience have you had with someone needing long-term care?"

   C. "Under what circumstances would you have to enter a nursing home as you age?"

   D. "What do you know about the cost of LTC in the area?"

4. Most people older than age 50 think an old person is someone how many years older than they are?

   A. 5

   B. 10

   C. 15

   D. 20

5. If the cost of LTC continues to increase at current levels, the cost will double every how many years?

   A. 5

   B. 10

   C. 15

   D. 20

5

Tailoring Policies To Meet Needs

A nother aspect of a suitable LTC insurance sale is matching the prospect's personal financial and family situations to the policy options. In other words, a suitable sale involves tailoring an LTC policy to the client's situation and needs. This tailoring process makes full use of the information contained in the fact-finder. Even with this information, however, the tailoring is prob ably the most difficult aspect of completing a suitable sale because so many variables must be taken into account.

Keep in mind that the agent doesn't make the decisions about how the policy is designed; the person who writes the check for the insurance does. The agent explains how each of the choices works, and then makes recommendations to his or her prospect. But the ultimate decision is left to the prospect. The agent will know the most suitable plan design has been made when the prospect becomes an applicant.

Suitability extends beyond the initial sale. Clients' personal situations and coverage needs can change over time. Agents receive commissions when policies are renewed to compensate them for providing ongoing customer service. And many clients need that agent service to update their coverage or to file a claim.

Agents should maintain contact with their clients to ensure that policy design choices continue to meet the clients' needs and budgets. The life of a senior takes many courses. If a client inherits a sizeable estate, for example, the client may want to add the additional coverage that he or she couldn't afford when the client purchased the policy. Or a client may have to take a new prescription that is expensive and not covered by Medicare or the client's Medicare-supplement insurance. As a result, the client may consider lapsing his or her long-term care coverage to pay for the medication. The agent, if he or she is available when needed, could reduce the coverage and premium rather than having the client lapse the entire policy. In most cases, some coverage is better than no coverage.

What is especially difficult about tailoring a policy to meet a prospect's needs is the fact that so much time usually passes between the time of purchase and the time of claim. Furthermore, the prospect is not likely to be the person who files the claim;

the children or spouse normally does. The suitability of a sale can change dramatically from the time of sale to the time of claim.

Typical sons and daughters of prospects want their parents to purchase as little coverage as possible. The premiums always seem too high for the intangible benefits. Chances are the annual premium is more than the children spent on their last vacation.

Sometimes children discourage their parents from buying LTC insurance. "Don't worry, we'll take care of you" is the refrain heard over and over when parents consult their children about purchasing LTC insurance. Unfortunately, the children may not be able to keep their promise to provide the necessary care because of the physical, financial or emotional stress involved in caring for a loved one. Children's attitudes about LTC insurance change dramatically when they file a claim for their parent. Now they want their parent to have more coverage. They frequently don't understand why the agent didn't sell their mom or dad a more comprehensive policy in the first place. If they complain to the insurance company, the agent may be asked to explain why the client purchased the type and amount of coverage he or she did. These types of issues have been known to show up in state insurance departments and on lawyers' desks and can escalate into lawsuits.

Because of these and other issues, it is important to keep detailed records on each client. Whether it is the client's children, the insurance company, the state insurance department or the courts asking the questions, documentation in the file will help answer their queries. Agents should make notes regarding conversations, particularly their recommendations and clients' decisions regarding important policy provisions. Agents should keep copies of the various rate quotes or illustrations they show clients. They never know when the additional documentation will protect them from fines or embarrassing situations in which their credibility is questioned.

The professional agent maintains errors and omissions (E&O) insurance. In the event a client wins a judgment against the agent, quality E&O coverage will pay the fine.

Finally, agents should keep in mind that prospects cannot be saved from their own decisions. Even with the best advice and experience available, many people choose not to listen. They make the decisions about how their LTC insurance is designed, and in doing so they may have some bias that cannot be overcome.

As an example, an agent can try to convince a prospect to purchase compound inflation protection because of its long-term cost-effectiveness. The prospect, however, will not add this valuable feature if he or she:

- doesn't think the cost of care will continue to increase 5 percent a year;

- wants to self-insure the rising cost of care;

- wants to purchase the additional coverage over the years (not expecting to ever become uninsurable); or

- simply cannot afford the additional premium.

When clients file claims, they often wish they purchased many of the benefits discussed at the time of sale. The problem is the same for anyone buying any insurance. You simply don't know whether you will file a claim. Prospects plan today for tomorrow's unknowns.

The agent's role in tailoring an LTC insurance policy to a prospect's needs is to:

- ask the prospect questions about his or her situation;

- explain the various choices and options; and

- make recommendations as to which options the agent thinks are best for the prospect.

The previous chapter provided guidance in obtaining needed information. This chapter helps agents use that information to make appropriate recommendations. It also provides tips on how to help prospects make appropriate decisions. When a sale is suitable, a client has an appropriate policy that pays the anticipated benefits when a claim is filed.

■ ■ ■ ■ ■

■ CHOOSING AN AGENT AND AN INSURER

First, a prospect must choose an agent and an insurance company. Both decisions are difficult because the prospect's relationship with each must be based on trust. How can that trust be established? An agent can begin building trust by showing genuine concern for the prospect's well-being and demonstrating knowledge about LTC insurance. The agent also builds trust by representing a credible company and a good product. That trust can be cemented if the prospect knows the company has a good reputation and is financially strong and stable. Various rating services publish the financial integrity and claims-paying ability of companies.

Another way an agent builds trust is by taking an educational and consultative approach to serving prospects. Prospects, like anyone else, want to be treated with respect, and treating prospects with respect involves giving them the knowledge necessary to make informed decisions when they purchase LTC insurance. Most of what prospects learn about long-term care and LTC insurance comes from agents and company-produced materials. Giving prospects objective and educational information empowers them to make informed decisions. It also shows respect for the prospects and their ability to learn and make decisions.

When prospects trust agents, they tend to listen to their recommendations and act on them. Such trust usually is nurtured over many years. When it develops quickly, it's often because an agent has been recommended highly by a prospect's close friend.

Consumer advocates advise people shopping for LTC insurance to meet with more than one agent and consider coverage from more than one company. The agent who takes an educational and consultative approach to serving prospects and shows a genuine interest in meeting their needs with LTC insurance builds the trust necessary to win in a competitive environment.

■ CHOOSING BENEFIT DESIGN OPTIONS

All companies offer essentially the same benefit design options. They may call them by different names, present different choices within the options or price some choices to sell more frequently than others. Some companies offer unique design features that get the same results more traditional design features obtain.

The merits of company practices and a discussion of every available option are beyond the scope of this text; however, it does provide a detailed analysis of the basic choices and options.

How can an agent understand how all options and choices fit every conceivable situation? It is impossible. When the agent has reached this part of the sales process, a suitable sale requires much more flexibility in the way the agent thinks. Designing a plan that a prospect agrees is right for him or her is an art, not a science.

It is impossible to design a matrix or a computer program that addresses all the variables involved in the decision-making process and results in the perfect LTC insurance policy. This can be accomplished only in the prospect's human brain after receiving information from many sources.

The options are addressed under three basic coverage design questions:

1. When are benefits paid?

2. How much is paid?

3. How long will payments continue?

■ WHEN ARE BENEFITS PAID?

Three things must happen before long-term care benefits are paid:

1. An impairment must exist.

2. Professional services must be received for the impairment.

3. The time for which services are received must be predetermined.

The contract language defines when an impairment exists; the prospect doesn't make that choice. The other two determinants become options for the prospect: the providers of care and the elimination period. Both provide the agents with an opportunity to use much of the information gathered in the fact-finding phase of the sales cycle to develop the agent's recommendation.

Providers of Care

Long-term care insurance policies cover:

- nursing facilities only;

- home care only; or

- a combination of nursing facilities and home care.

Nursing Facilities Only

Including coverage for care in a nursing home is essential to a suitable sale. Why? Because nursing home care accounts for the largest out-of-pocket expenditures for most people needing long-term care. Although most people prefer the luxury of receiving care in their homes, for many it eventually becomes infeasible. Few people in nursing homes today ever expected to be there, and probably no one wanted to move into a nursing home when the subject was first discussed. Nevertheless, for many, it is where they receive the most appropriate and cost-effective treatment. Usually, after people have been in a nursing home for a while, they develop friendships and participate in activities that were not available at home.

The most popular LTC insurance policy covers nursing home care. Such policies also provide benefits for care received in assisted living facilities, adult foster care homes, residential facilities and facilities with other names, as licensed by the states in which the insurance is purchased. Nursing home insurance continues to evolve to encompass more types of facilities that provide less intensive care than that provided in nursing homes. Claimants are happy to know they can enter more than one type of facility and still receive benefits. Including these alternate providers of care in a prospect's plan is very important because more and more people are living in these types of facilities for as long as people once stayed in nursing homes. In fact, these alternative settings are what people today expect when they consider aging.

Home Care Only

Benefits payable for care received at home are on most people's wish lists when they initially discuss LTC insurance. People who buy this type of coverage have a strong desire to stay in their homes regardless of the circumstances. Once they see the premium this option adds to the coverage, however, many settle for facility-only policies.

Many argue that home care is much more cost-effective than care in a nursing home. This is true when someone needs part-time care—maybe to help the person bathe and dress in the morning, and then change into sleepwear for the evening. The individual pays for just the care received, not for the room and board charges built into a facility's invoice. Professional home care is most useful when it supplements an informal caregiver. In this case, the professional works in the home for a few hours, up to a full eight-hour shift. This gives the informal caregiver a break to address his or her other responsibilities. Replacing the informal provider requires around-the-clock care, which is beyond the scope of most LTC policies. However, when professional assistance is needed 24 hours a day, the cost of home care soars.

Consider a full-time provider who charges $10 per hour (which, in many parts of the country, is impossible to find), or $240 per day. Just about any nursing home can provide excellent care for this amount of money. However, the cost of home care insurance that provides $240 per day is exorbitant for most people. This is why having coverage for care in a facility makes so much sense.

Insurance companies cover community-based providers other than home care agencies. Common examples are assisted living facilities and adult day care centers. Services such as respite care and hospice care are also covered. Agents should know all providers covered under the home care option and explain them to prospects.

Home care insurance makes the most sense when a prospect's family or friends live nearby and provide some of the care. All sorts of things during the day and night may require assistance, such as preparing a meal, taking medications, using the bathroom or telephone and moving from room to room. As discussed above, having professionals around the clock to provide this type of care can be expensive. Family or friends do it out of love for the person in need of help.

Most people dread going to a nursing home for care. Some prospects refuse to even consider the possibility. They would rather die than live in a nursing home. The last thing they want is for their children to get the money from an insurance company to pay for their care in a nursing home. They're afraid that as soon as they're slightly impaired, their children will cart them off to an old folks home because the insurance benefits make it possible. For these prospects, a suitable sale might be a home-care-only plan. The drawback the prospects should know about is that insurance benefit payments stop when they no longer can receive care at home because their caregivers are physically, emotionally or financially exhausted. Again, most people in facilities did not plan to live there or even want to live there.

Another type of suitable home-care-only sale is to someone who already owns a nursing facility policy. Rather than replacing the older policy, adding stand-alone home care insurance creates a comprehensive combination. The prospect must understand that the two policies work independently of one another.

Nursing Facilities and Home Care

An increasingly popular choice in LTC sales is the comprehensive coverage that provides benefits in a facility and in the community. Although more expensive than either of the stand-alone choices, this plan gives the claimant many choices of service providers and, thus, more control over the quality of care he or she receives. For prospects in search of complete peace of mind regarding their long-term care insurance, a comprehensive plan is the best option.

Documenting conversations with prospects, particularly agent recommendations and decisions prospects make, and servicing clients on a regular basis are critical activities. Well-documented client files come in handy if problems arise. (It is very easy for a home-care-only claimant to accuse his or her agent of wrongdoing if the claimant must enter a facility and insurance benefits are no longer available.) Staying in contact with each client may result in an opportunity to add facility coverage to a home-care-only plan if a life-changing event occurs (for example, a friend enters a facility and reports that it isn't all that bad).

Needs Assessment

In assessing the type of coverage suitable for a prospect, an agent can ask the following questions for insight:

- **As you become old, how do you want to be cared for?** The answer to this question helps the agent determine the appropriateness of home care insurance. If the prospect says, "I'd like my kids to help out," the agent should try to learn more about the children. Are they willing and able? If so, the agent might recommend home care coverage. Home care is also suitable when a spouse will provide care. If the prospect says, "I'd rather not burden my children. I'll go to Shady Acres on the west side of town," the agent knows home care coverage isn't that important to the prospect.

- **Do you have family or friends nearby who will care for you if you need care at home?** If the prospect answers no, home care may not be appropriate. Even so, if the prospect insists on home care, the agent should recommend that the policy be designed to cover part-time care. If the prospect answers yes, the agent should find out whether the proposed caregiver is willing and able to take care of the prospect. Has the prospect discussed this expectation or made arrangements with the proposed caregiver? The agent should recommend maximizing the home care benefit if the prospect has planned to receive care at home. This question need not be asked of a couple who plans to care for each other.

- **Does your proposed caregiver work outside the home?** If so and home care is appropriate, the prospect needs coverage for at least eight hours a day while his or her caregiver is at work. A policy with adult day care service benefits is another alternative.

- **Does your caregiver still have children living at home?** If the proposed caregiver is still raising his or her children, providing care to the prospect adds a new set of responsibilities. Being part of the *sandwich generation* (caring for younger children and older parents simultaneously) is stressful for all involved. Balancing everyone's needs with the right insurance coverage is not easy.

- **How many hours a day would you like someone to come in to help you so your caregiver can take a break?** If the answer is just a couple of hours a day, the agent should design the home care so it covers four hours of care. Full home care benefits are appropriate when the prospect says, "My caregiver works during the day, so I would need someone here while he (or she) is at work."

- **Do you think you could pay $50 per day (the cost of a couple hours of home care) for someone to care for you at home without putting a huge dent in your budget?** If the prospect answers yes, he or she may want to consider self-insuring some of the cost of home care. If the answer is no and receiving care at home is a viable option, the agent should add the coverage.

Elimination Period

The elimination period is the number of days an insured pays expenses before his or her LTC policy begins to pay benefits. Other terms used include *deductible* and *waiting period*. The elimination period begins when the claimant meets the criteria for benefit qualification (with a TQ plan, this is when the claimant is chronically ill) and begins receiving covered services. Each carrier has its own definition of the elimination period, and some companies have one elimination period for home care and another for nursing home care.

In a suitable sale, the agent explains to the prospect how the option works. Some insurance companies count each day of care as one day against the elimination period. Some count one day (or two or three days) of home care as a week (or seven days) against the elimination period. Some consider days of care received in the home to be separate from days of care received in a nursing facility.

When explaining how the elimination period works, agents must understand this product intricacy thoroughly. They should be sure to explain what happens when someone receives, for example, three days of home care per week:

- Does it count as three days of home care? If so, it will take 10 weeks to satisfy a 30-day elimination period.

- Does it count as a week (seven days) of home care? If so, it will take four weeks and two days to satisfy a 30-day elimination period.

Companies offer different elimination periods, so an agent can design a plan to meet every prospect's situation. Each choice is expressed in a number of days. No company offers all the choices, so many agents like to have a couple different company plans available. The common choices follow:

- 0 days

- 15 days

- 20 days

- 30 days

- 60 days

Many prospects understand the elimination period better when it's expressed in dollars. For example, a 20-day elimination period where the cost of care is $175 per day equates to an out-of-pocket cost of $3,500 at claim time; a 90-day elimination period with a $140 daily cost of care is a $12,600 deductible; and a 365-day wait with a $125 daily cost results in a $45,625 payment before the insurance begins to pay. Some insurance companies are experimenting with basing the elimination period on a dollar amount rather than a number of days.

When considering the costs of elimination periods, an agent and a client must consider current as well as future costs. If nursing home costs continue to increase at 5 percent a year (the validity of this assumption is discussed later in this chapter), the cost of care will double every 15 years.

ILL. 5.1 ■ *Age and Cost of Care*

Age	Cost of Care Per Day	90-Day Elimination Period
40	$125	$11,250
55	$250	$22,500
70	$500	$45,000
85	$1,000	$90,000
100	$2,000	$180,000

Let's look at an example. Bill Thompson, a 40-year-old carpenter, is considering buying an LTC policy. The cost of care in an LTC facility in Bill's area today is $125 daily, and that cost is expected to double about every 15 years. Consequently, by the time Bill turns 55 years old, the cost of care could be $250 per day. At age 70, care could cost $500 per day. When Bill is 85 years old and most likely to need care, it could cost $1,000 per day. If Bill is lucky enough to reach 100, the cost could double again to $2,000 per day.

Let's assume Bill is considering a 90-day elimination period, which is the equivalent of an $11,250 deductible. This could grow to a $90,000 out-of-pocket payment at age 85. No one knows for sure how the cost of care will continue to increase or how much a dollar will buy in 30 or 50 years, but prospects should be made aware of how inflation will affect their elimination periods.

Prospects' risk tolerance and financial resources determine the right elimination periods for them. Agents must look for the indications. If prospects have high deductibles on their homeowner's and automobile insurance, they probably will want short elimination periods. If they own one of the more comprehensive Medicare-supplement plans, they probably will want to minimize their out-of-pocket medical costs and likely will want to do the same with their long-term care insurance. If they have large retirement nest eggs, they probably will want to self-insure much of the initial costs of long-term care and opt for longer elimination periods.

The one way to be sure how a prospect feels is to ask him or her questions that make the prospect think about his or her situation and what is important to the prospect.

Needs Assessment

Answers to the following questions will help an agent determine and recommend an appropriate elimination period for a prospect:

- **Do you carry low or high deductibles on your homeowner's and automobile insurance?** If the prospect carries low deductibles, the agent should recommend a short elimination period because the prospect probably likes to minimize out-of-pocket costs. If the prospect has high deductibles, the agent should recommend a long elimination period because the prospect likely prefers to self-insure the costs up front.

- **Do you want to pay for the first few months of your care, or will you need help after the first few weeks?** If the prospect wants to pay for a few weeks, the agent should recommend a short elimination period. If the prospect wants to pay for a few months, the agent should find out how many months—three, six, twelve? The agent can make the prospect's answer his or her initial recommendation.

- **How much have you set aside for your long-term care costs?** The agent then divides the amount by the average daily cost of care to get the number of days the prospect is willing to self-insure. An alternative to this plan is to place the money saved in an annuity to pay the higher LTC insurance premiums that accompany a shorter elimination period.

- **Would you like to reduce your current premium with the understanding that you will have to pay more out of pocket if you happen to need care?** This question helps the prospect understand the trade-off between the cost of care and the premium—the premium is reduced as the elimination period is lengthened. The prospect's answer will guide the agent in his or her recommendation.

■ HOW MUCH IS PAID?

Two components comprise how much money a claimant receives: the daily maximum benefit amount the claimant applies for initially and the type of inflation protection the claimant chooses. The claimant makes one choice for today, and the other, for the future.

Daily Benefit Amount

The daily benefit is the maximum amount of money a policy will pay each day at the time of claim. The prospect decides how much he or she wants when the prospect applies for the coverage.

In determining the benefit amount best for a prospect, an agent must know the cost of nursing home care and other LTC services in the area and how much a prospect can and is willing to contribute each day to pay for his or her care, if anything. The difference between the cost of LTC and the amount the prospect is willing to contribute, if anything, is the benefit amount the prospect should choose.

The best agent knows the cost of care in the area in which the prospect lives. This information helps the agent make an appropriate recommendation; it also gives the prospect confidence in the agent's ability to help the prospect make the right decision. The prospect looks for someone to trust when purchasing long-term care insurance. When the agent knows something as simple as the cost of care at nearby facilities, the prospect grows to trust the agent. The more the agent knows, the more confidence he or she instills in the prospect.

The typical cost of long-term care is easy to obtain. For starters, the Yellow Pages list nursing homes and other LTC facilities. The agent should call a few, or better yet, visit them. Most will show visitors around the facilities and provide materials listing current costs. Many administrators are happy to meet with insurance professionals, because they view LTC coverage as the facilities' best source for revenue in the future.

The agent can pick up copies of the newspapers published specifically for seniors in grocery stores, bookstores and pharmacies. These usually are free because of the amount of advertising they contain. The agent then can call some of the advertised facilities—nursing homes, assisted living facilities and so forth—to learn about them.

When continuing care retirement communities (CCRCs) and assisted living facilities open, they often hold open houses. The agent should take advantage of these opportunities to better understand the types of providers available in the community.

The Yellow Pages also list home care agencies. When the agent calls some of these, he or she should ask questions about the cost of care from the agencies' various professionals—nurses, aides, physical therapists and so forth. The agent should understand what a typical home visit entails and get a sense of how Medicare has affected the home care business. It is amazing how quickly agents learn about care providers by talking to a few of them.

Each insurance company has minimum and maximum daily benefit amounts it offers applicants. The minimum normally is the lowest level a state insurance department allows (or the company is willing to accept), and the maximum usually is the highest level the company believes is appropriate for a given geographic area.

Companies also set different maximum daily amounts based on providers. They may offer 50 percent, 75 percent and 100 percent of the nursing home daily maximum for home care. Another choice might be either 75 percent or 100 percent of the nursing home daily maximum for care in a facility other than a nursing home. Some offer reimbursement up to a single daily maximum regardless of who provides the care—100 percent of the nursing home daily maximum for all providers.

Agents must explain to prospects how benefits are paid. Is it monthly, weekly or even bimonthly? Are prospects reimbursed for actual charges, or do they receive flat dollar amounts regardless of the cost of care?

Reimbursement Plans

A reimbursement plan considers the actual services a claimant receives from various providers. After reviewing a copy of the bill sent in by the claimant's financial advisor, the company considers whether the services received are considered qualified under the policy. (The Health Insurance Portability and Accountability Act of 1996 [HIPAA] defines qualified services for tax-qualified plans, and most companies use language directly from this legislation.)

If the services received are covered, the charge for the services is reviewed. If the amount owed is less than the daily maximum, the claimant receives an amount equal to the actual cost of care. The difference between the daily maximum and the actual charge is "saved" in the benefit maximum for future use. (How the benefit maximum works is discussed later in this chapter.)

ILL. 5.2 ■ *Reimbursement Plans*

	Out-of-pocket cost for insured	Amount credited against benefit maximum
When actual charge is less than the maximum daily benefit	None	Actual charge
When actual charge is equal to the maximum daily benefit	None	Daily maximum
When actual charge is greater than the maximum daily benefit	Charges above daily maximum	Daily maximum

If the amount of the actual charge covered under the policy equals the daily maximum, the full daily amount is paid. When the cost of the services is the maximum daily benefit, the claimant pays the amount of the charge that exceeds the policy maximum.

A situation where the claimant exceeds the daily maximum for home care three days a week and does not use it fully the other four days can create frustration for the claimant. Some companies offer a feature allowing a claimant to receive reimbursement for actual charges that exceed the policy's daily maximum. In this case, the company sets a weekly or monthly rather than daily maximum benefit.

Let's consider a policy with a home care daily maximum of $100. A nurse provides care three days a week for $125 per day; an aide charges $50 a day to provide services for the other four days of the week. A policy with a daily maximum reimburses $100 when the nurse cares for the claimant and $50 when the aide does— a total of $500 per week. A policy with a weekly maximum reimburses $125 for the nurse services and $50 for the aide services—a total of $575 per week. The weekly maximum in this example equals seven days times $100 per day, or $700. Given the above assumptions, this claimant could maximize the policy values by receiving care from the nurse four days a week (4 days × $125 = $500) and from the aide another four days (4 days × $50 = $200). The informal caregiver could enjoy a restorative break on the day when both the nurse and aide deliver care.

Indemnity or Per Diem Plans

Indemnity plans work differently than reimbursement plans. An indemnity plan pays the full daily benefit maximum regardless of the actual charges. The policy might have different daily maximum levels for different providers. Where and the frequency with which the claimant receives the care is considered, but actual charges are not evaluated at claim time with an indemnity plan.

Using the above home care example, a claimant owning an indemnity plan receives $100 per day ($700 for the week) when care is delivered as long as a professional provides the care. When the nurse charges $125 per visit, the claimant pays the extra $25 out of pocket. When the aide charges $50 per visit, the claimant can use the extra $50 of insurance benefits to cover the nursing services or other expenses. For example, the claimant could use it to pay the informal caregiver or keep the extra money in an account to pay for nursing or other care in the future.

One thing possible under an indemnity plan that is not possible under a reimbursement plan is coverage for an uninsurable spouse. In this case, the healthy spouse buys twice the daily benefit appropriate for today's cost of care. Then, if both the husband and wife need care at the same time, the insured spouse's additional benefits help offset the cost of care for the uninsurable spouse.

Designed properly, both the indemnity and reimbursement designs cover a prospect's cost of care. Keeping all other factors constant (which cannot happen in today's LTC insurance market), the reimbursement plan is a little less expensive. The trade-off for the lower premium, however, is that the claimant must submit actual invoices or bills to the insurance company. The indemnity plan requires notice that care has been received rather than how much it cost. Claim processing likely will proceed more quickly with an indemnity plan.

In a suitable sale, the agent explains whether the long-term care insurance coordinates with Medicare. A tax-qualified indemnity plan *can* coordinate, but a tax-qualified reimbursement plan *must* coordinate with Medicare. A nontax-qualified plan is not bound by any such restrictions.

A company can coordinate with the actual reimbursement of Medicare or not pay any amount when Medicare pays. In 2000, Medicare's skilled nursing care copayment is $97 per day; that is, Medicare pays the charges exceeding that amount. The company coordinating with actual reimbursement pays the $97, whereas the "any/none" company pays nothing. The difference won't matter for those claimants owning good Medicare-supplement plans covering both skilled nursing copayments and at-home recovery.

Prospects should know how the daily benefit is paid whether they buy reimbursement or indemnity plans. Explaining how the daily benefit works is a suitability requirement for agents, and it makes prospects feel more comfortable with the policies. Furthermore, prospects who feel comfortable with how the insurance works are more likely to become applicants.

Needs Assessment

Determining an appropriate level of daily benefit is difficult. Knowing the typical cost of care in an area is important, but it's not enough. As with the elimination period, the agent must understand both the risk tolerance and financial resources of the prospect. There are really two ways to design a daily benefit amount:

1. full-cost-of-care plan

2. copayment plan

ILL. 5.3 ■ *Assessing a Prospect's Daily Benefit Amount Needs*

Common Living Expenses

- Mortgage/rent $_____/month
- Utilities $_____/month
- Food $_____/month
- Insurance $_____/month
- Taxes $_____/month
- Transportation $_____/month
- Medical expenses $_____/month
- Other expenses $_____/month

Total living expenses $_____/month

Plus Nursing Home Costs $_____/month

Equals Expenses When Care Is Needed $_____/month

Less Common Sources of Income

- Pension $_____/month
- Social Security $_____/month
- Savings/Investments $_____/month
- Other $_____/month

Total Income $_____/month

Equals Minimum Monthly LTC Benefit $_____/month

The full cost of care is simple to understand. If a nursing home charges $130 per day, for example, the prospect buys $130 worth of coverage per day. This approach appeals to many consumers—especially those who want to minimize their out-of-pocket expenses. The drawback is that the insurance premium under this plan is more than it is under the copayment method.

People who like the full cost of care approach usually carry low deductibles on their homeowner's and auto insurance. They also typically have more expensive Medicare-supplement plans that include coverage for the Part B deductible. These people would rather pay an insurance company a little more each year to be sure they don't have to sell assets to pay deductibles.

The copayment plan is a more creative approach to designing a daily benefit amount. It looks at a prospect's income and expenses to determine how much remains to cover the cost of care. By lowering the daily maximum benefit amount in creating the copayment, the prospect lowers the LTC insurance premium.

Illustration 5.3 shows how an agent can assess a prospect's daily benefit needs. The science is in determining the minimum coverage using actual charges; the art comes in when the agent works with the client to determine the correct copayment. This chart can be used during the fact-finding process or when discussing benefits to determine the daily benefit to recommend.

Asking questions helps the agent better understand the prospect's views and, thus, enables the agent to make a better recommendation. Some examples follow:

- **Do you carry low or high deductibles on your auto and homeowner's insurance?** The agent can use the answer to this question to determine both the deductible and copayment on the LTC plan. Prospects with low deductibles usually want coverage for the full cost of care. Prospects with high deductibles generally want to keep the cost of their insurance low; consequently, they are attracted to the copayment plan.

- **How do you feel about using some of your own income to pay for your care?** Prospects frequently need an explanation before answering this question. The chart in Illustration 5.3 is especially helpful. The prospect who wants to use some of his or her own income is more likely to purchase long-term care insurance with a copayment plan. The prospect who doesn't want to use any of his or her excess income most likely will want a full-cost-of-care plan.

- **Would you like your insurance benefits to cover the full cost of care or just a portion?** This is simply another way to ask the prospect whether a full-cost-of-care plan or a copayment plan makes the most sense.

- **Do you prefer a plan that will pay a flat dollar amount regardless of the actual cost of care or one that simply reimburses you for actual charges?** The agent should ask this question only if he or she can offer both types of plans—indemnity and reimbursement. It boils down to how the prospect wants his or her claims paid.

- **Do you know how needing care might affect your budget?** If the prospect doesn't, the agent should use the worksheet in Illustration 5.3.

- **Do you want a plan that will pay tax-free benefits, or are you willing to risk that your benefits will be taxed?** This question addresses the tax-qualified and nontax-qualified issue discussed in Chapter 2. If the agent only sells one type of plan, the agent should explain why he or she prefers one to the other. This discussion will help if the prospect decides to seek recourse against the agent because the prospect made the wrong decision. In a courtroom, a client can claim ignorance and accuse an agent of negligence if the agent fails to discuss this issue.

Increasing Benefits

The cost of care has risen over the years, mostly due to inflationary pressures, additional regulatory reporting requirements, the increasing complexity of care delivered and rising wages in nursing homes. Illustration 5.4 shows projected costs of nursing home care through 2040. The cost of nursing home care has increased by about 5 percent a year over the last decade and a half. Home health care costs have risen at a much slower rate—close to 2 percent. The Consumer Price Index expanded in 1998 to include nursing home and home care. This will help agents better track the cost increases, but it is still important for the agents to monitor the costs in their areas.

> ### ILL. 5.4 ■ *Projected Costs of Nursing Home Care*
>
> | Year | Annual Cost | Daily Cost |
> |------|-------------|------------|
> | 2000 | $48,000 | $130 |
> | 2010 | $78,000 | $215 |
> | 2020 | $125,000 | $340 |
> | 2030 | $205,000 | $560 |
> | 2040 | $338,000 | $925 |

If the cost of nursing home care continues to increase at 5 percent a year, the buying power of a client's LTC insurance will erode every year the client owns it—unless some form of inflation protection is added. At 5-percent increases, the cost of care doubles about every 15 years. (As with all inflationary measures, nursing home cost increases are based on the previous year's costs. In other words, they are compounded every year.)

For a 55-year-old considering LTC coverage, nursing homes likely will charge four times today's rates if he or she needs care at the typical age of 85. Based on today's average yearly cost of about $48,000 and 5-percent increases over time, Illustration 5.4 indicates how the cost of care in a nursing home could increase over the next 40 years.

Prospects have four ways to offset rising costs:

1. self-insure;

2. purchase additional coverage;

3. begin automatic simple increases; or

4. begin automatic compound increases.

Research indicates that self-insuring is the option most LTC insurance buyers select—by default. Because they are not willing to pay the added costs for other available options, they in essence self-insure the rising costs of long-term care.

For example, consider someone who buys a policy today without inflation protection that pays $130 in daily benefits. If that person needs care in 10 years, he or she must pay the difference between the $130 and, say, $215 (using Illustration 5.4); that is, the insured pays $85 out of pocket each day he or she needs care. The insurance helps offset some of the cost, but not all of it. Some people find this a perfectly acceptable alternative. Children filing a claim usually find the situation intolerable.

Purchasing additional coverage over time is a good alternative for people who are unsure whether they'll keep the coverage or who anticipate their budgets changing in the future. Some of the people who seem likely to self-insure actually try this option to keep pace with inflation. The challenge with this alternative is maintaining one's good health so underwriting is not an issue. Unfortunately, we all enjoy our good health on a day-to-day basis and never know when it will take a turn for the worse.

Some companies offer a feature that allows insureds to purchase more daily benefits without evidence of insurability. This purchase option may be available every two or three years. Some companies require that each option be exercised otherwise future options are no longer available. Some companies allow more flexibility. But none of them, however, allows an insured to accumulate options. The dollar amount of the purchase option varies. It could be based on a set dollar amount, a predetermined percentage of the original daily benefit or a component of the Consumer Price Index. The full option may need to be exercised or just a portion of the option amount. A company might cap the total amount of the purchase options or set an age when it no longer makes offers to purchase. Any option requires additional premiums based on the amount purchased at the insured's attained age. These technical aspects of the purchase option are explained to the prospect in a suitable sale.

Purchase options work well for people who want full control of their LTC insurance. They will want to analyze the cost of care when an option is made and purchase an appropriate amount of coverage.

Nothing is wrong with this pay-as-you-go mentality, though it does have risks:

- The additional insurance may become unaffordable.

- The cost of care may increase faster than the amount available through the purchase options.

- The options no longer may be available because of the prospect's age or because the prospect has purchased the maximum coverage.

A person also may purchase additional coverage when he or she takes out the initial coverage. In this case, the insured purchases twice the current daily cost of care or the insurer's maximum daily benefit. This works well when the insured goes into claim status in the first 15 years of the policy. (In areas where the cost of care is already higher than average, a company may not allow the purchase of such a high daily maximum.)

For the person who enters claim status 30 years after he or she purchases a policy that includes double coverage (a 55-year-old needing care at age 85, for example), the insurance protection erodes to half its purchasing power. Isn't it ironic that the insured was fortunate not to need care for many years, but unfortunate in that the insurance can't do what the insured wanted it to do when he or she purchased it?

Automatic increase riders are the best inflation hedges to own, but the most expensive to purchase. The insured pays a higher initial premium with the understanding that the premium will not rise as benefits increase. (Premiums are adjustable, as with all guaranteed renewable contracts.) Each year, the insured's daily benefit is increased, usually by a predetermined percentage, while the premium remains unchanged. This option simply prepays for future benefits.

ILL. 5.5 ■ *Simple Benefit vs. Compound Benefit Increase Options*

Policy Year	Daily Benefit with SBIO (5% Simple Increases)	Daily Benefit with CBIO (5% Compound Increases)
1	$100	$100.00
2	$105	$105.00
3	$110	$110.25
4	$115	$115.76
5	$120	$121.55
10	$145	$155.13
15	$170	$198.00
20	$195	$252.70
30	$245	$411.61

The most popular increase is 5 percent. Companies have the option of offering amounts either higher or lower. Some companies have experimented with options based on components of the Consumer Price Index.

Two types of automatic increases exist:

1. simple

2. compound

Simple increases are based on the increases in the original daily benefit. Compound increases use the previous year's daily benefit as the basis of the increases. Simple increases take 20 years to double, while compound increases take just 15. Illustration 5.5 shows the difference in dollar amounts.

According to HIPAA and the NAIC's model regulation, the 5-percent compounded annually option must be offered to all prospects. Every company that sells LTC insurance makes this option available. Unfortunately, not enough people choose it because they're not willing to prepay future benefits.

As illustrated above, nursing home costs have risen about 5 percent a year since 1987. If costs continue to escalate at the same pace, those who decided to self-insure the inflated portions of their long-term care costs may be in for a surprise when they need care eventually. The suitability of a sale may well come under scrutiny when a client's children file a claim.

ILL. 5.6 ■ *Pay-As-You-Go vs. Prepayment Plans*

	Age							
	55	**60**	**65**	**70**	**75**	**80**	**85**	**90**
Pay-As-You-Go Plan								
Daily Benefit (purchasing additional coverage)	$100	$130	$165	$210	$265	$340	$410	$410
Cumulative Premium	$512	$3,502	$7,861	$14,884	$27,515	$52,398	$100,047	$155,152
Prepayment Plan								
Daily Benefit (with 5% compounded annual increases)	$100	$128	$163	$208	$266	$339	$433	$552
Cumulative Premium	$1,080	$6,480	$11,880	$17,280	$22,680	$28,080	$33,480	$38,880

This compares the cost effectiveness of a long-term care insurance contract that purchases additional coverage (pay-as-you-go) with automatic increases (prepaid). The amounts of annual increases are consistent but not exact because the pay-as-you-go option is limited to purchases in $5 increments.

In the first year, both plans offer $100 per day. The prepayment plan costs about twice as much as the pay-as-you-go plan.

As the insured ages, the daily benefit increases about the same under both options. The pay-as-you-go plan is purchasing additional coverage at an ever-increasing age. We assume the insured remains insurable. Also, unless the company offers an option to increase benefits during a claim, the pay-as-you-go option will not increase in benefits during a claim.

The cumulative premium of the two plans has a cross over in cost effectiveness between ages 70 and 75 in this example. In other words, if the insured lives beyond age 75, prepaying for the additional increases will be the most cost-effective way to purchase additional coverage.

Finally, the cost of care will not stop increasing when someone turns age 85. But most insurers do not offer the coverage after ages 79 or 84, so the opportunity to purchase additional coverage is limited. With the prepaid option, the increases continue until death or lapse regardless of age.

For people who plan to keep their coverage in force more than 15 or 20 years, the 5-percent compounded annually method is the most cost-effective way to buy LTC insurance that keeps up with rising nursing home costs. Prospects must understand that LTC insurance is a classic example of "you get what you pay for."

Illustration 5.6 illustrates the cost-effectiveness of the 5-percent compounded annually feature. The professional agent runs through this same sort of analysis using his or her favorite company's regular rates and rates with compound inflation. The company may even make this analysis part of its illustration system.

Agents should remember this about the 5 percent compounded annually option: it is painful to buy, but great to own.

Needs Assessment

Successful presentations focus on needs and benefits. An excellent way to begin a dialogue on the inflation option is to ask the following questions:

- **How long do you plan to keep this coverage?** Typically, the prospect expresses disbelief that the agent is even asking such a question, or he or she will answer "Until I die." The purpose of the question is to get the prospect to realize he or she will keep the coverage until death. If the prospect cites a time span that seems too short, the agent should ask the prospect why he or she feels that way. This information helps the agent understand the prospect's personal beliefs so the agent can make a good recommendation. Those who plan to keep their coverage 15 or more years (usually the younger prospects) should consider seriously the prepayment alternative. People who plan to lapse their coverage as soon as they get that big inheritance so they can self-insure the entire cost of their long-term care should not prepay future benefits.

- **How much do you think nursing homes will charge when and if you need one?** No one knows for sure how much care will cost when he or she needs it; however, this question makes the prospect realize the cost of care will continue to increase—no matter when the prospect plans to use the benefits. Telling prospects that the cost of long-term care doubles about every 15 years helps them understand how much care might cost in the future.

- **How do you anticipate paying for that care?** The prospect should start to be concerned about not only the cost of care today, but also the cost of care in the future. This question is very effective in getting younger prospects to open their minds to the idea of having insurance to offset the rising cost of care. If they think self-insuring against inflation is the way to go, this series of questions may help them realize how expensive that can be over the long run.

- **Would you be interested in an option that enables you to keep up with rising costs?** This question lets the prospect know there is a solution to the problem the agent identified with the previous three questions. Without specifying the merits or cost of the insurance alternative, the agent can use the picture the prospect just painted in presenting the solution. The prospect plans to keep the coverage, the cost of care will be high and the prospect has no other alternative to offset rising LTC costs. If the prospect is interested in the insurance option, the agent will best serve him or her with an explanation of the benefits of each of the methods available to offset inflation. Discussion of price comes much later.

- **How do you feel about paying additional amounts now for additional future benefits?** This question helps the agent understand whether prepaying future benefits makes sense to the prospect. Some prospects feel comfortable with this concept—they have ample cash flow to pay the premiums and want to buy their coverage once and not think about it for a long time. Some are unsure of the value of prepaying future benefits and want to manage their insurance benefits closely. Remember, the applicant makes the decisions.

- **Do you feel you'll be able to afford the additional coverage in the future?** This question should be asked of prospects who decide the pay-as-you-go option is best for them. The question not only addresses a prospect's budget, it also helps the prospect recognize there is added cost in the future. Maybe the prospect is expecting an inheritance, an investment is maturing or the prospect plans to sell his or her rental property to provide additional income in the future. Maybe the prospect currently supports a child or parent, will pay off his or her mortgage or is in the process of reducing other expenses that will create additional disposable income to pay for the increasing benefits. The only way to be sure is to ask!

Everyone's situation is different, which is one reason insurance companies offer so many alternatives to offsetting the rising cost of long-term care. To make a suitable sale, an agent must take time to understand the nuances of an individual's or a couple's personal and financial situations, then explain the alternatives.

The agent should keep an open mind when discussing the alternatives. What the agent considers expensive may not be to a prospect. By asking the prospect questions, the agent tries to learn what is important to the prospect.

Helping prospects understand the problem in today's as well as tomorrow's dollars helps them make purchasing decisions they will feel comfortable with for the long term. And when a claim is filed, the benefits paid are the ones the client expected when he or she purchased the coverage.

■ HOW LONG WILL BENEFITS CONTINUE?

The final choice a prospect must make concerns how long he or she wants benefits to continue. The LTC insurance company limits its risk by setting a maximum exposure it is willing to accept. It is no different with other types of insurance.

Benefit Maximum

The benefit maximum is the total number of days for which a policy pays benefits or the total dollar amount the policy pays. An indemnity or a per diem plan normally counts the number of days (pool of days), while a reimbursement plan counts the amount of money (pool of money) paid to the claimant.

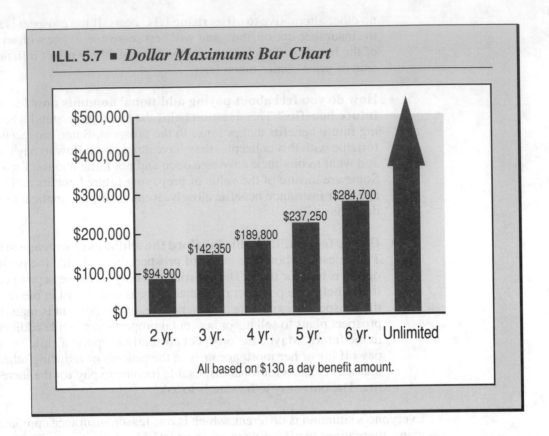

ILL. 5.7 ■ *Dollar Maximums Bar Chart*

All based on $130 a day benefit amount.

The benefit maximum should not be confused with the maximum daily benefit amount. Although the two work together, they are separate choices, independent from one another.

The choices for the benefit maximum normally are expressed in years. Common options include two, three, four and six years. Most companies now offer unlimited maximums. The unlimited plan is just that—no maximum amount is payable. The claimant who still needs care never receives a final check.

The total number of days available is determined by multiplying the number of years chosen by 365. Therefore, a three-year plan has 1,095 days available for a claim. A claim with a pool of days maximum reduces the maximum number of days remaining by one for each day benefits are paid.

The total dollar amount available is determined by multiplying the number of years chosen by 365 by the daily benefit amount. Therefore, a three-year plan with a $130-per-day maximum has $142,350 available for the claimant ($3 \times 365 \times 130 = 142,350$). The dollar amount benefit maximum is reduced dollar for dollar when the claimant is paid for services received.

The total amount available increases when a policy includes inflation protection. In this case, the maximum available is recalculated each year using the new daily maximum. The insured is rewarded for having had the foresight to add a 5 percent compounded annually inflation protection rider.

Needs Assessment

Which benefit maximum should an agent recommend? It isn't an easy question to answer. An agent concerned with making a suitable sale asks the prospect questions, listens carefully to the answers, explains the different options, then makes a recommendation and waits for the prospect to select an option. The agent follows the same steps in dealing with all the major options. Following are some questions the agent can use to gather the information the agent needs to make his or her recommendation:

- **Do people in your family live long lives?** Many prospects think they will live as long as their ancestors lived. Sometimes this is true, but in most cases there is no correlation. Some believe Alzheimer's disease is passed from generation to generation, although no clinical evidence proves this. Because the prospect makes the decisions, the agent should find out whether the prospect thinks life expectancy is hereditary. People who think they will live long lives generally are interested in long benefit maximums.

- **Has any member of your family spent a long time in a nursing facility?** Some prospects think that because their parents, aunts, uncles or grandparents needed long-term care, they, too, will need it someday. This question helps the agent learn from the prospect whether the prospect thinks a correlation exists from generation to generation. It also helps the agent understand the prospect's motivation in wanting to discuss the LTC insurance option. If a close relative of the prospect needed care for a couple of years or longer, it won't take a lot of convincing to make the prospect understand the value of longer benefit maximums.

- **Do you want to cover the average stay in a nursing home or are you more concerned with the financial risk an extended stay in a nursing home poses?** Many people want to protect against an average stay in a nursing home of about three years, but almost as many people stay longer than the average as stay shorter than the average. There is no sense trying to convince prospects that few "average" people exist. Agents must let them make their own decisions. If an average stay is what concerns a prospect, he or she will want a shorter benefit maximum.

- **Do you feel a benefit maximum of $_____ (insert the amount the prospect is considering) will cover an average stay when you most likely will use it?** This question builds on the questions asked earlier regarding the cost of care in the future and whether the prospect wants to add inflation protection. The agent uses the query to help the prospect understand the limitations of the shorter benefit maximums, especially if the prospect has decided not to add the inflation protection. After thinking this concept through, many prospects gain additional insight into the importance of inflation protection. Others continue to request one of the shorter benefit maximums.

- **When do you want your last check?** This summarizes what the prospect actually must consider when selecting a benefit maximum. The last check is the one sent to the claimant when the benefit maximum expires. The prospect could receive his or her last check after three years, six years or whatever other option the insurance carrier offers. The prospect also can choose a plan that guarantees the prospect won't receive a last check as long as he or she continues to need care and obtains it from a health care professional. The guaranteed no last check option is the unlimited maximum most carriers offer today. Many prospects want their benefits to continue indefinitely, while others are comfortable with receiving their last checks after three years in a nursing home (anticipating that the stays will be average).

■ ADDITIONAL OPTIONS AND CHOICES

By this time, the agent should have a good perspective on the major issues involved in designing a suitable LTC policy for the prospect. The agent obtained that perspective by weighing the answers to the following three questions:

- When are benefits paid?

- How much is paid?

- How long will payments continue?

The answers to these questions guide the agent in designing the prospect's LTC policy. While the following additional options are not essential to an LTC plan, they may enhance the insured's satisfaction with the coverage.

Nonforfeiture Options

Some prospects, particularly those who have purchased life insurance that builds cash values, want to get something back if they don't use the coverage. Prospects who don't own life insurance or have purchased only term insurance in the past are not as concerned about receiving a refund.

Regarding a tax-qualified (TQ) plan, HIPAA specifies what can be returned to an insured who lets his or her coverage lapse. Premium refunds and dividends can be used only to reduce future premiums or to increase future benefits. A death benefit also is allowed.

An agent selling a TQ plan must propose a nonforfeiture benefit. The one every company offers allows for a shortened benefit period if the insured lapses his or her coverage after the third year. The shortened benefit period minimum is 30 days (90 days in California); the maximum is the total premium paid over the life of the policy divided by the daily benefit amount at lapse. When the nonforfeiture benefit becomes effective, the daily benefit is locked in, any inflation protection is removed and the elimination period cannot be changed.

A nontax-qualified (NTQ) plan sets no restrictions on what can be returned. The insurance can generate cash values that build over time and are given to the insured when he or she lapses the policy or to the heirs when the insured dies. If a company desires, an NTQ plan could allow the insured to borrow against the cash values.

Needs Assessment

The following questions guide agents in assessing the suitability of a nonforfeiture option.

- **How long do you plan to keep this coverage?** The agent asked this question earlier, when discussing the inflation option. If the prospect answered something other than, "Until I die", a nonforfeiture option may make sense to the prospect.

- **Are you concerned with getting something back if you have to lapse your coverage?** The prospect is usually the one asking a version of this question, and the nonforfeiture option is the answer. It is far from perfect, though, providing limited benefits. Companies price the option in relation to the likelihood it will be used and the amount of benefit that will be paid. It's usually not expensive.

Husband and Wife Features

Some couples complain about the need to buy policies for both the husband and the wife, so various companies have come up with innovative ways of addressing this concern. Different methods have been developed so a husband and wife can benefit from each other's policy.

The original spousal benefit involves waiving premiums on the healthy spouse's policy when the other spouse becomes a claimant. This is designed to give the healthy spouse peace of mind because his or her policy won't lapse while the other spouse receives benefits.

A few companies offer plans that give couples the option of accessing each other's benefit maximum. If both husband and wife take out plans with three-year benefit maximums and one spouse uses up his or hers, that spouse, in a claim situation, can access the healthy spouse's benefit maximum. If both were to take out unlimited maximums, however, they wouldn't need to worry about accessing each other's maximum.

A survivorship benefit rewards the widow or widower for the continual premium payments of the deceased spouse. If an insured dies after a specified number of years (usually about 10), the surviving spouse no longer must pay premiums on his or her LTC insurance.

HIPAA concerns arise when these spousal features are added to TQ plans. A TQ plan cannot pay benefits unless the insured is chronically ill. HIPAA is silent on the issue of benefits taken from a healthy spouse's policy and given to a chronically ill spouse. Consequently, these options may jeopardize the tax-favored status of a TQ plan. Agents offering these options must inform prospects of this risk.

One way to ensure TQ status is to combine both husband and wife on one policy. Benefits can be paid to a chronically ill spouse regardless of the other spouse's health status, and premiums for the entire policy can be waived even though one spouse remains healthy.

Some companies offer a combined policy when one spouse cannot qualify medically for coverage on his or her own. The uninsurable spouse is added to the insurable spouse's policy. Benefits are paid to the unhealthy spouse only after the formerly healthy spouse goes into claim status.

One feature that does pass HIPAA scrutiny is a spousal discount because this establishes a new class of insureds. A percentage decrease of premium is available for both husband and wife. Companies have different definitions of what has to happen for a couple to qualify for the discount. Some say both must apply for coverage; some say both must be issued coverage; some say both must have their coverage in force.

In any event, an agent shouldn't worry about assessing the need for a spousal discount feature. Everyone is willing to accept a lower premium for the same benefits offered by the same company if it is available.

Companies build various caveats into these features that prospects must be aware of before deciding whether the features are for them. All husband and wife benefits are ancillary features designed to fulfill wants, not needs, or are available only when other insurance alternatives are not. Therefore, needs assessment questions are not necessary.

■ SUMMARY

The art of designing a plan that meets all of a prospect's wants and needs takes time to master. This chapter cannot explain exactly how to accomplish it. A computer program cannot be designed to do it. Developing a matrix or chart is not possible.

It takes hard work with many prospects for an agent to master the art. It takes an ability to learn from one's mistakes when a sale isn't made. It takes learning to ask the right questions in various situations. It takes listening skills to better understand prospects' concerns and values. It takes knowledge of companies' products. It takes an understanding of the cost/benefit trade-off of each policy design choices. It takes concern for prospects' best interests.

Wisdom sets in when an agent has mastered the art of designing a plan that fulfills needs and makes the prospects want to purchase it. This is a milestone in the quest for suitability, which achieves its ultimate goal when an insurable event occurs and a policy performs as the client expects.

■ CHAPTER 5 QUESTIONS FOR REVIEW

1. Which of the following is NOT one of the agent's roles in tailoring an LTC insurance policy to a prospect's needs?

    A. Make policy design decisions for the prospect

    B. Ask the prospect questions about his or her situation

    C. Explain the various policy choices and options

    D. Make recommendations about which options the agent thinks are best for the prospect

2. A 365-day elimination period where the cost of care is $125 a day results in which of the following payments before insurance begins to pay?

 A. $30,325

 B. $38,625

 C. $45,625

 D. $48,325

3. Under a reimbursement plan, what happens when the cost of a service is greater than the daily benefit amount?

 A. The claimant receives an amount equal to the cost of care.

 B. The claimant pays exactly half of the cost of care, and the insurer pays the other half.

 C. The claimant receives an amount equal to the full daily benefit maximum, regardless of actual charges.

 D. The claimant pays the amount of the charge that exceeds the daily benefit maximum.

4. Which of the following statements is true of the person who writes the check for insurance?

 A. He or she makes all policy design decisions.

 B. He or she makes policy design decisions with the agent.

 C. He or she makes some policy design decisions.

 D. He or she delegates all policy design decisions to the agent.

5. The total number of days for which a policy pays benefits is called the

 A. benefit maximum

 B. elimination period

 C. daily benefit

 D. per diem

6

Completing the Application and Serving Clients

O nce an agent and a prospect agree on which LTC insurance options make the most sense and the premium is acceptable to the prospect, an application is completed. LTC insurance applications are not as simple to complete as the preapproved credit card applications everyone receives these days —and for good reason. The LTC risk for an insurance company is significant, whereas the risk of loss with a credit card is limited. For example, an LTC insurance claim for a patient with Alzheimer's disease could cost a company $250,000 to $500,000 or more. A credit card has a much lower financial exposure—a preapproved credit limit of $5,000, for instance.

As with a credit card, a mortgage loan or other forms of insurance, underwriting is a necessity because everyone buying insurance or applying for a loan wants the best deal available. To offer that deal, the underwriter of credit or insurance must find a risk pool similar to the applicant.

If the insured is less of a risk than those in an available risk pool, the insured subsidizes the people in that pool. In other words, the insured overpays for his or her coverage. If the insured is more of a risk than the majority of those in an available risk pool, the insured does not pay his or her fair share. When the underwriter finds the right risk pool, the insured pays an amount just right for his or her risk. Although this may sound a little like the situation in *Goldilocks and the Three Bears*, risk management is serious business.

Consider automobile insurance. Everyone wants to pay the lowest premium for the right amount of coverage. An independent auto insurance agent shops a client's risk with multiple companies, looking for the right risk pool and a fair rate. Automobile insurance underwriting considers the driver's age, gender, marital status and driving record, as well as the type and age of the car. A 16-year-old male with two speeding tickets driving a new sports car pays a high premium. Furthermore, a 50-year-old married couple with perfect driving records wouldn't want to be in the same risk pool as that 16-year-old because they would have to pay a significantly higher premium than necessary.

The same concept applies to LTC insurance. A 60-year-old marathon runner is better off in a risk pool with other healthy individuals than in a pool of people with Alzheimer's or Parkinson's disease. It is the LTC insurance underwriter's job to pool like risks after reviewing applicants' health histories. Some companies have one risk classification, issued, while others have many classifications, such as preferred, select, choice and standard, or table A, B and C, and so forth. The LTC agent is responsible for understanding the risk selection process and classification systems of various companies and for placing clients in risk pools that reflect their health histories.

Some agents have their clients apply for coverage with more than one company. They know the preferred rate with company A is better than the standard rate with company B. On the flip side, company A accepts only the healthiest people in its preferred risk class, and its standard rate is not as good as company B's standard rate. Rather than wondering whether their clients are healthy enough for the preferred rate at company A, the agents apply to both companies to ensure that coverage is available from either one of them.

Without underwriting, there would be no need to plan, no need to purchase insurance ahead of time. When an insurable event occurred, a person simply could call the insurance company for money. A widow could ask for $500,000 worth of life insurance on her recently deceased husband without paying a premium and expect to receive it. When someone entered a nursing home, he or she could call the insurance company and ask for $130 a day to cover costs. All of this is absurd, of course, but it demonstrates the importance of underwriting and planning before an insurable event occurs.

In this chapter we'll examine the important processes of underwriting, completing the LTC insurance application and serving the client.

■ ■ ■ ■ ■

■ LTC UNDERWRITING

LTC underwriters try to determine who is likely to need care in the near future. They look for life-style choices, injuries or illnesses, such as progressive degenerative diseases, that lead to a loss of independence and a need for LTC services.

Someone who sits on a couch all day watching television, drinks alcohol to excess and smokes three packs of cigarettes a day is not making choices that are likely to result in a long and healthy retirement. Chances are the person's health will deteriorate to the point of needing care in the future. On the other hand, a person who volunteers at the blood center, humane society and church, travels extensively, eats healthy meals, plays tennis and walks a couple of miles a day most likely will enjoy a long, healthy retirement. The latter scenario describes the type of risk an LTC underwriter likes to take.

Some injuries, such as a strained muscle, lead to a temporary loss of independence. Other injuries, such as an automobile accident that results in multiple broken bones and a loss of memory, cause serious long-term damage. Underwriters look for the cause of injuries and the extent of recovery to determine whether they should offer insurance coverage.

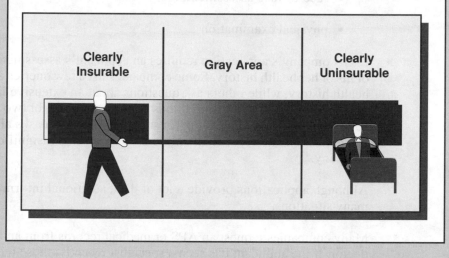

ILL. 6.1 ■ *Continuum of Insurability*

The underwriter's challenge is considering the health histories and lifestyle choices of applicants in the gray area and then placing them in the right risk pool. Just like selling long-term care insurance, underwriting is an art, not a science.

| Clearly Insurable | Gray Area | Clearly Uninsurable |

Certain illnesses make underwriters nervous; others have no effect on their decisions. Someone who recently suffered a heart attack, for example, causes anxiety for an underwriter, while a person who had a heart attack six years ago, is now physically active, and has taken his or her medication religiously is a much better risk.

Frequently, applicants have extensive histories of multiple conditions for which they've received treatment. Some applicants take many different prescription medications for various ailments. An underwriter must understand how these conditions and medications affect each other and the likelihood of their leading to the need for long-term care services.

Progressive degenerative diseases are the biggest challenge for an underwriter and agent. Some companies feel an insulin-dependent diabetic is a safe risk, while other companies automatically decline such an applicant. The same is true for people with arthritis, emphysema, multiple sclerosis, hearing and vision impairments and heart conditions. Agents provide the best service to prospects when they apply for coverage with the companies most likely to accept their types of risk at fair rates.

LTC insurance is underwritten at the time of application. Underwriters consider information from a variety of sources, including the following:

- application

- attending physician statement (APS)

- applicant's medical records

- Medical Information Bureau (MIB)

- AIDS or HIV test

- personal history interview

- face-to-face assessment

- physical examination

Each company's application requires an applicant's assessment and understanding of his or her health history. Some companies list a few queries about the applicant's health history, while others ask questions about an extensive list of medical conditions. Some inquire about conditions that existed a year or two ago, while others go back 10 years or more. Striving for suitability, an agent asks all of the questions on an application and records all answers. No answer is insignificant to an insurance company.

Although applications provide a lot of data, additional information is necessary in many situations.

Many companies request an APS or medical records from an applicant's primary doctor. If the applicant has seen a specialist recently, those records are reviewed also. Frequently, the application and the medical records are not consistent, for the following reasons:

- The applicant did not tell the agent about a medical condition for which the applicant received treatment (all an agent can do is ask the questions and expect honest answers).

- The agent didn't think the condition was significant, so he or she didn't record it on the application (in a suitable sale, the agent records all answers the applicant gives).

- The applicant did not know of a medical condition. Perhaps the doctor told the applicant to take a prescription medication to feel better, but didn't tell the applicant about the underlying condition. Or without knowing it, the patient/applicant may be on a drug to help slow the progress of a chronic condition, like memory loss.

Is this inconsistency between the application and medical records a mistake, an omission, negligence or fraud? The agent should not try to find out. Using such labels can damage a person's reputation and result in a loss of trust between the agent and insurance company or the agent and applicant. More serious cases caused by agent error can result in a loss of appointments with companies or a revocation of an agent's insurance license. Nevertheless, underwriters must investigate and resolve such issues before deciding whether to offer coverage.

Agents work for both applicants and insurance companies. They must balance the needs of both, even when those needs conflict. Sometimes they feel stronger allegiances to applicants, especially when they have known the applicants for many

---

ILL. 6.2 ■ *Agents as 'Field Underwriters'*

Agents were formerly known as *field underwriters*. Although the term is lost today, top agents still provide that service. In doing so, they furnish personal pictures of applicants for home office underwriters. Agents meet applicants, talk to them, watch their actions, and, in most cases, see the environments in which they live. An observant agent helps a home office underwriter by providing this information in the agent's report section of the application or in a separate memo. When an underwriter is uncertain whether to issue coverage, an agent's report can make the difference between rejection and approval.

---

years. Going to bat for an applicant is appropriate, but going so far as to bring an agent's integrity into question is going too far. Honesty and full disclosure are always the best ways for an agent to conduct business.

An agent must record all answers an applicant gives and must ask for a list of the applicant's prescription medications. One suggestion for obtaining an accurate list is to ask the applicant to bring each prescription to the meeting table. Then the agent knows all are listed and spelled correctly on the application.

Another source of underwriting information is the Medical Information Bureau. The MIB is a nonprofit agency that serves as a central source of reliable information on the medical histories of insurance applicants. The MIB helps disclose cases where applicants either forget or conceal pertinent underwriting information or submit erroneous or misleading medical information with fraudulent intent. The bureau is supported by more than 700 member insurance companies. Agents should tell applicants that medical information is available to insurance companies through the MIB, and it might be accessed for underwriting purposes.

Although AIDS has not resulted in significant LTC insurance claims, some companies worry about that possibility. These companies have found that just requesting HIV/AIDS tests reduces the number of applicants whose lifestyle choices put them at risk of AIDS. To these companies, the money they save on claims for this disease justifies the cost of saliva or blood screens HIV/AIDS.

Two other sources of information on an applicant's health are the personal history interview and the face-to-face assessment. The interview is conducted usually over the phone, while the assessment is performed at the applicant's home or office. They both attempt to gain additional insight into the applicant's health history. Trained professionals ask questions designed to assess the applicant's overall health, including his or her ability to complete tasks healthy people take for granted and the ability to think, perceive, reason and remember.

Each company's underwriting standards define the circumstances under which the company uses these additional sources of information. The most common reason is age. Everyone older than a certain age receives a face-to-face assessment regardless of his or her medical history. Agents must tell prospects what tests they must undergo and emphasize the importance of taking them seriously. Many applicants have been denied coverage because they answered the questions carelessly. The best agents never let this happen with their applicants.

Some applicants have not visited their doctors in a long time. This is cause for concern at some companies, especially if the applicant is of an advanced age. Such applicants may be asked to see a physician for a routine physical examination. An alternative is to have a nurse visit the applicants to check vital signs and draw blood for analysis.

Each of these assessments costs time and money. Doctors charge for completing attending physician's statements, copying medical records and sending them to insurance companies. Sometimes, a specialist is listed in a person's medical records when the specialist wasn't disclosed on the application. The specialist's records then must be ordered and the specialist paid for his or her services. Although an insurance company employee usually conducts the personal history interview, the company must compensate the employee and pay for the employee's work area. Most companies use nurses in applicants' cities for face-to-face assessments.

Waiting for medical records, assessments and test results takes time. Obviously, the more documents ordered, the longer the wait. Usually, it takes between one and four weeks to obtain the information necessary; then the underwriter needs a couple of days to decide whether to offer coverage.

An agent can facilitate the underwriting process by disclosing all physicians and specialists the applicant has seen within the number of years the insurance company requests. Some companies allow agents to request (not take receipt of) records from physicians. Everyone involved—underwriters, applicants and agents—gets frustrated when the underwriting process is delayed.

Underwriters have difficult jobs. They must assess each applicant's medical history and current functional status to determine whether the applicant likely will remain independent for an extended period of time. If so, the applicant is offered coverage. If not, coverage is denied.

■ COMPLETING THE APPLICATION

The agent is responsible for completing the application—obtaining all required information, including signatures—and providing all disclosure documentation. This is accomplished in meetings with the applicant.

The application, with the applicant's and agent's signatures, becomes part of the policy, which is a legal contract. By signing the application, both the applicant and agent attest to the fact that all the information in the application is true. Mistakes or omissions, whether or not intentional, expose the agent or applicant to legal liability. Negligence or fraud is a frequent claim in legal proceedings. An agent who has asked all the required questions while sitting with an applicant, recorded all the answers, obtained all the necessary signatures and furnished all disclosure documentation can provide strong evidence in his or her defense should questions arise.

When completing the application, the agent must take the following steps:

- **Provide all of the information requested, leaving no question unanswered.** The agent can ensure that he or she has done this by reviewing all paperwork in the prospect's presence and again at the office.

- **Complete the application in the applicant's presence.** When working with an existing client, an agent can obtain some information (such as date of birth, Social Security number, address and so forth) from the client's file. However, it is always best to confirm this information with the client. It is never appropriate (or legal) to have an applicant sign a blank application, then phone the applicant to ask the questions and record the answers.

- **Record all information as provided by the applicant.** If information is unclear or appears to conflict with other information, the agent should attempt to resolve the discrepancy before submitting the application. The agent should verify facts and obtain any additional information needed. Any lingering discomfort is best documented in the agent's report section of the application.

- **Commit to providing accurate information.** The agent should obtain a list of common medical conditions and prescription medications from the insurance company. This list is valuable in resolving uncertainties, avoiding confusion and providing correct spellings of conditions and drugs. The list probably will identify conditions that make applicants unacceptable risks. If an applicant has one of these conditions, the application process should cease.

- **Strive to reduce unintentional lapses.** The agent should obtain the name and address of a trusted individual to receive a billing notice if the policy is about to lapse. Many companies offer this option on their applications, while some states require companies to make it available. With a suitable sale, obtaining this name is important. In addition, the person listed is a possible prospect for long-term care insurance.

- **Obtain necessary signatures.** Long-term care coverage requires more disclosure and signatures than many other forms of insurance. When an agent takes applications on both a husband and wife, it is important to obtain the correct person's signature on the correct application.

- **Complete the agent's report.** This includes information about the agent's relationship with the applicant and the applicant's habits and general character.

- **Complete the suitability statement.** Many companies require an assessment of each applicant's method of payment and estimates of financial resources. It may seem intrusive, but it protects agents and the companies from future recourse in claims of inappropriate sale.

- **Provide the applicant with the outline of coverage.** All state insurance departments require that each applicant for LTC insurance be given an outline of coverage. This is a very brief description of the policy's most important features. The form contains disclosures as to what the policy does not cover and how to qualify for benefits. Some applicants use the outline of coverage to compare policies. Given its standard format in each state, it provides an overview that is reasonable for comparison purposes.

- **Give the applicant a copy of the NAIC's** *A Shopper's Guide to Long-Term Care Insurance.* This guide, a required disclosure document in most situations, is available from all insurance companies.

- **Provide all receipts and documentation according to the laws of the state and the requirements of the insurance company.** All companies provide this information to agents. Agents who represent multiple insurers must review and understand the nuances from company to company.

Failing to follow these procedures delays the underwriting process. Most home office underwriting departments return applications with missing answers or require additional disclosure documentation when the policies are delivered. Either cause of delay is avoidable if agents adhere to details when completing applications.

■ NAIC'S SUITABILITY GUIDELINES

The National Association of Insurance Commissioners (NAIC) developed and adopted a *Long-Term Care Insurance Model Act* and a *Long-Term Care Insurance Model Regulation* to curb the sale of LTC insurance to individuals who should not own it. Insurers are asked to establish standards for suitable sales. Section 21 of NAIC's model regulation states "The agent and insurer shall develop procedures that take the following into consideration:

- the ability to pay for the proposed coverage and other pertinent financial information related to the purchase of the coverage;

- the applicant's goals or needs with respect to long-term care and the advantages and disadvantages of insurance to meet these goals or needs; and

- the values, benefits and costs of the applicant's existing insurance, if any, when compared to the values, benefits and costs of the recommended purchase or replacement."

Each insurer is asked to develop an LTC insurance personal worksheet, a model for which is contained in NAIC's *Long-Term Care Insurance Model Regulation* (see Appendix A). At a minimum, this worksheet must consider the premium amount, the premium payment source and a range of the applicant's assets and income. The applicant also is given the NAIC's "Things You Should Know Before You Buy Long-Term Care Insurance," a list also contained in NAIC's *Long-Term Care Insurance Model Regulation* (see Appendix B). With help from the agent, the applicant uses the worksheet and the list in making his or her decision to purchase the coverage.

Working with consumer advocates, the NAIC established these guidelines for suitability:

1. Premiums should not exceed 7 percent of income.

2. If an applicant wishes to purchase the coverage for asset protection, he or she should have at least $30,000 in assets.

Although these are reasonable guidelines, it is still up to each applicant to decide whether the coverage is suitable. As with all decisions regarding policy options, suitability decisions also reside with applicants.

According to national surveys conducted by the Health Insurance Association of America and LifePlans, Inc., in 1990 and 1994, most people who buy LTC insurance have annual incomes of less than $35,000. Close to a third also have assets of less than $30,000. On average, buyers of LTC insurance spend 6 percent of their household income on their LTC insurance policy.

LTC insurance is suitable under circumstances other than those listed above. For example, if a child pays the premium on a policy, the 7 percent criterion is irrelevant. And as long as they don't have to reduce their budget for such necessities as food, clothing and shelter, some people don't mind spending more than 7 percent of their income on LTC insurance for the peace of mind the coverage gives them. Finally, some applicants purchase LTC coverage for reasons other than asset protection. For example, many people buy the insurance so they can choose where they receive care or to avoid depending on ever-changing government programs.

When an applicant doesn't meet an insurer's guidelines for suitability and still wants to apply for coverage, the insurer sends the applicant a letter documenting the fact that the applicant doesn't meet the insurer's suitability standards. The insurer then gives the applicant the choice of purchasing or not purchasing the policy. Again, the final decision rests with the applicant.

It is important to note that not all states require this suitability documentation; nevertheless, many insurers recognize the value of documenting suitability. In the long run, the insurer, applicant and agent all benefit from completing the paperwork required to take this one-time, static snapshot of an LTC policy's financial suitability for the applicant.

■ THE INITIAL PREMIUM

Companies offer agents and applicants two ways of applying for long-term care insurance: with the initial premium paid or with the initial premium due upon policy delivery. Each method has important implications:

- When an agent collects the initial premium from a prospect with the application, coverage begins on the date of the application as long as the applicant is insurable under the insurer's underwriting guidelines.

- When an agent does not collect the initial premium, coverage begins on the issue date, after the insurer receives the first premium. Disclosures must be made of any changes to the applicant's health history from the time of application to the time of issue, when the company collects the initial premium.

If an applicant has a condition that would make him or her uninsurable, the coverage never is considered to be in force, regardless of whether the agent collected the initial premium with the application. Let's say, for example, an applicant paid the initial premium with the application, then was in an automobile accident that left her in need of LTC care before the policy actually was issued. If the applicant's medical history at the time of application was such that the company would issue her the insurance, she would qualify for benefits. If this applicant had not paid the initial premium, she would not qualify for coverage because her health history changed between the time of application and the time of issue.

A sticky situation arises when an applicant experiences symptoms he or she does not disclose to the agent that lead to uninsurable health, but the health problem has not been diagnosed by a doctor at the time of application. If the health problem is diagnosed during the underwriting process, the condition is assumed to have existed at the time of application because the symptoms were present.

Market Conduct Issues

A conditional receipt is given to every applicant who pays the initial premium with the application. The receipt stipulates that a conditional contract is formed between the insurer and the applicant. It is conditional because it is contingent on the premise that the applicant is, in fact, insurable and the policy will be issued as applied for. Therefore, if the underwriting process determines that the applicant is uninsurable or insurable only with a higher premium or fewer benefits, no contract actually exists unless and until the applicant agrees to the new terms the insurer has offered.

The agent must read and understand the conditional receipt, then explain it to the applicant, emphasizing when coverage is in force as described in the receipt. This agreement can vary from one company to another; therefore the insurance company must address any uncertainties or questions the agent has regarding it.

The conditional receipt raises market conduct issues. Many applicants who want to pay the initial premium don't understand that coverage is in force only after the insurance company receives the initial premium. For this reason, diligent agents will do the following:

- neither state nor imply that coverage is in force when an application is completed and submitted (Implying that coverage is in force when it isn't is one of the primary causes of complaints and lawsuits against agents and insurers. Agents must take responsibility for explaining clearly how the conditional receipt works.);

- give a conditional receipt only to an applicant who pays the initial premiums (Diligent agents don't provide conditional receipts when applicants promise that their checks are in the mail or will arrive at a future date, and they certainly never accept post-dated checks.); and

- provide each applicant who submits the initial premium with the conditional receipt, then take a few minutes to explain how the conditional receipt works. (Reading the document to the applicant is the easiest and safest way to communicate the information.)

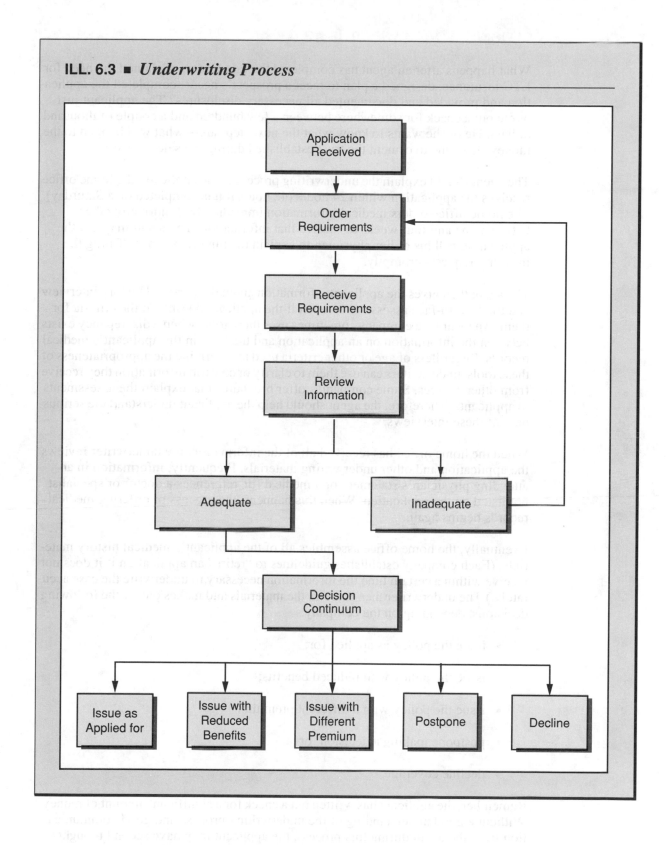

ILL. 6.3 ▪ *Underwriting Process*

▪ CLOSING WORDS WITH THE APPLICANT

What happens after an agent has completed the fact-finder, explained the need for LTC insurance, designed a plan to meet a prospect's needs, completed the application and provided and documented all necessary disclosures? The applicant just wrote out a check for somewhere between a few hundred and a couple of thousand dollars. He or she wants to know what the next steps are—what will happen to the money! It's time to cement the trust established during the sales process.

The agent should explain the underwriting process to the applicant: the home office receives the application within 24 hours (48 hours if it is completed on a Saturday). The home office orders medical information immediately. It normally takes between one and four weeks to receive that information. The agent may ask the applicant to call his or her physician to explain the importance of fulfilling the insurer's requests promptly.

The agent then gives the applicant information about the personal history interview and the face-to-face assessment—even if the applicant doesn't fit the criteria for them. An insurance company sometimes uses these tools when a discrepancy exists between the information on an application and the facts in the applicant's medical records. Regardless of age or other criteria used to determine the appropriateness of these tools, underwriters can use them to clarify or confirm information they receive from other sources. Some companies offer brochures that explain the assessments to applicants. Therefore, the agent should help the applicant understand the seriousness of these interviews.

When the home office has received all of the information, the underwriter reviews the application and other underwriting materials. Frequently, information in an attending physician's statement or a medical file references a doctor or specialist not listed on the application. When this happens, the process of ordering medical records begins again.

Eventually, the home office assembles all of the applicant's medical history materials. (Each company establishes guidelines to "retire" an application if it does not receive within a certain time the information necessary to underwrite the case accurately.) The underwriter then reviews the materials and makes one of the following decisions, depending on the company:

- issue the policy as applied for;

- issue the policy with reduced benefits;

- issue the policy with a different premium;

- postpone making a decision; or

- decline coverage.

Remember, the applicant has written out a check for a significant amount of money. Without a good understanding of the underwriting process and good communication from the agent during this process, the applicant may have second thoughts about the purchase decision during the four to six weeks it takes the underwriter to make a decision about the application.

> ## ILL. 6.4 ■ *Activities in which Agents Should Never Engage*
>
> 1. Sign an applicant's name or trace an applicant's signature on anything
>
> 2. Witness an invalid signature (such as a wife signing for a husband) or sign as a witness to a signature the agent has not seen take place
>
> 3. Write on or highlight a policy, an outline of coverage or an illustration; make marks on any of these documents
>
> 4. Make promises or guarantees beyond a company's documented promises and guarantees; put anything in writing or make verbal statements that guarantee premium payment arrangements, the likelihood of changes to the premium in the future, a likely underwriting outcome and so forth
>
> 5. Alter any of the application materials (An agent often finds an unanswered question when reviewing an application back at the office. When this happens, the agent should take the necessary time to meet with the applicant again to get the question answered properly.)
>
> 6. Endorse checks made payable to the agency, broker-dealer, company or insured
>
> 7. Commingle client funds by cashing checks or holding funds belonging to the client or company
>
> 8. Share commissions with the insured (Agents should not offer rebates or provide anything else of value as an inducement to purchase coverage.)

■ BACK AT THE OFFICE

Much of ethical conduct involves little more than establishing a system for keeping complete and accurate records and documents and processing paperwork promptly. Because the application is such an important document, one that becomes an actual part of the insurance contract, it is important to review it for completeness. This simple step helps avoid delays in the underwriting process. An agent should consider having a staff member review it—new eyes tend to notice different things. If additional information is needed from the applicant, the agent shouldn't let the application linger incomplete. Also, the agent shouldn't schedule a time to meet with the applicant for just a few minutes to finalize the documentation before sending it to the insurer.

Once all documentation has been completed and reviewed for accuracy, the agent must initiate the underwriting process immediately. Applicants expect, and have a right to expect, their applications to be processed promptly. Agents can facilitate the process by working with a sense of urgency to get the decisions made on the applications as soon as possible. They can demonstrate this sense of urgency by making personal commitments to have the applications in the mail to the insurers within 24 hours of taking them (48 hours if taken on Saturday). This is what applicants expect. Anything less disappoints and frustrates them and undermines the trust relationships they have established with their agents.

Once the application has been submitted, the agent should establish a pending file that includes a copy of the application and other forms submitted to the insurer, along with an illustration showing the amount of coverage applied for and the premium calculation. Underwriting status reports the agent receives from the company should be kept in this file, also.

These administrative steps are crucial and cannot be overlooked or managed casually. Many agents hire someone to manage this process for them so they can focus their efforts on contacting and meeting more prospects. Whoever does the work should do it well because it's an essential component of a suitable sale and benefits all parties involved—applicant, agent and insurer. Efficient and effective administration accomplishes the following goals:

- **It ensures timely policy issue.** Actively monitoring the underwriting process and communicating with the applicant reduce the possibility that the client will refuse the policy when it's offered.

- **It provides a foundation for growing the agent's business.** The agent with a couple of hundred clients is glad he or she established effective administration procedures when the agent started the business.

- **It enables the agent to stay in business longer.** Good records protect the agent from frivolous complaints, lawsuits and market conduct concerns.

- **It meets the agent's ethical responsibilities.** Well-documented files allow the agent to provide the prompt and courteous service that clients expect and deserve.

■ ONGOING COMMUNICATION

The insurer likely will provide information to the agent regarding the status of the underwriting process. The agent may find that weekly calls to the applicant to share this information enhances trust and, thus, reduces or eliminates buyer's remorse.

The following provide partial scripts for such calls:

- "The home office has received your application and has ordered medical records. Have you thought of any more questions about the coverage you've applied for? Have you been contacted to arrange your personal history interview or face-to-face assessment?"

- "The home office is still waiting for your medical records. Dr. _____ [the agent should take the name off the copy of the application] probably has the request by now. If you have a minute today, would you please call his [or her] office and ask the staff to process _____'s [the insurance company's] request as soon as possible? Have you had your personal history interview or face-to-face assessment?"

- "The home office has received your medical records and should have a decision on your application in another couple of days. When I hear, I'll call you to schedule a time to get together." Or, "The home office is still waiting for your medical records. Did you have a chance to call Dr. _____'s office? How did your face-to-face assessment or personal history interview go?" Or, "It appears Dr. _____'s records were not adequate, and the insurance company is ordering additional records. How did your personal history interview or face-to-face assessment go?"

- "I have good news for you. Your coverage has been issued just as we asked. I should have the actual policy in the next couple of days. When is a good time for me to bring it over to you?" Or, "Remember when we discussed the range of possible underwriting decisions that could occur? Well, your medical history has resulted in a change in the coverage. Let's discuss it. When is a good time for us to get together?"

It's important for the agent to be positive during all communications with the applicant. For example, making disparaging remarks about the timeliness of the home office serves no purpose. Such remarks can create doubt in the applicant's mind about whether he or she really wants a policy from that company, decrease the trust the applicant has in the agent, create an opportunity for the applicant to register a formal complaint against the insurer or result in a withdrawn application and lost sale. Remember, the applicant has a few hundred to a couple of thousand dollars entrusted with the insurer. Now is not the time for the agent to instill a negative attitude in the applicant.

If delays occur in the underwriting process, the agent should explain the problem simply and honestly. The agent should let the client know that delays are frequent in this business because:

- it takes time for doctors to fulfill insurance companies' requests for information;

- medical records are not always complete; and

- some records refer to other doctors or specialists not previously known, which means added time to contact them and obtain their records.

The agent should help the applicant understand the importance of the underwriting process. Remember, it's all designed to place the applicant in the proper risk class so everyone within the group pays his or her fair share in premiums for the coverage.

Finally, when talking with the applicant, the agent should support the underwriter's decision. Again, disparaging remarks serve no purpose except to undermine the confidence the applicant has in the agent and insurance companies in general. If the agent doesn't like the company's decision, he or she can appeal the underwriter's decision or submit an application with another insurer. If the agent decides to appeal the underwriter's decision, he or she should work directly with the insurer, using logic or new medical information to change the decision. The applicant need not know this is going on. Underwriters have a responsibility to combine like risks, basing their decisions on medical information that indicates how the applicants function around their homes and in their communities.

■ POLICY DELIVERY

Once the insurance company decides to accept the risk, it issues a policy. Prompt delivery of the policy is a good business practice. According to HIPAA, the policy must be delivered to the insured within 30 days. Therefore, prompt delivery is a legal requirement as well as good business.

How will anyone ever know whether an agent delivers a policy on time? A lot of things can happen to tip off the applicant, and sooner or later, they usually do. For example, another agent could meet with the client to review his or her coverage. This agent will want to review the actual contract language to make a suitable comparison. If the policy isn't available, a complaint can be filed against the original agent with the state insurance department. The resulting investigations can lead to a loss of license, a monetary fine or another form of reprimand, all of which damage the agent's reputation.

The best opportunity to go through the policy with the insured is when it is delivered. Without marking the policy, the agent should explain:

- the disclosures on the cover page;

- the schedule of benefits;

- how the policyowner qualifies for benefits;

- conditions excluded from benefits;

- how a provider of care is defined;

- how to file a claim; and

- why the application is attached.

During this explanation, the agent should listen for cues from the client about items that could cause concern—if not now, maybe in the future. The agent should address these concerns and assure the client that the policy he or she just purchased will serve the client's needs for many years to come. Also, the agent should remind the client that the agent will make sure the client receives the level of continued service he or she expects.

■ SUMMARY

The administrative side of the insurance business is the most difficult for many agents. Whereas the sales process offers many opportunities for creativity, the application and underwriting processes have many set rules that agents must follow. Problems and delays occur when the agents do not understand or do not carry out properly procedural details.

The agent represents both the insurance company and the applicant. This can cause situations in which the agent tries to bend the rules just a little to benefit his or her friend who has applied for coverage. (A prospect quickly becomes a friend of the agent after spending a couple of hours discussing personal matters.) When agents feel potential conflicts of interest arise, they must adhere to company guidelines and help their clients understand why it is so important to follow those rules. Honesty and full disclosure are always the best courses of action.

It is impossible to know all policies and procedures for all insurance companies; however, it's essential for an agent to understand the underwriting processes for his or her primary companies. Even then, the agent should do his or her best to work through the mishaps that occur and learn from them. Maintaining a positive attitude during this struggle makes it easier for everyone involved in the administrative process.

Underwriting is an essential component of all types of insurance. The pooling of like risks ensures minimal and stable premiums for those buying LTC insurance.

■ CHAPTER 6 QUESTIONS FOR REVIEW

1. If an insured is more of a risk than the majority of people in an available risk pool, which of the following statements is true?

   A. The insured subsidizes the other people in that pool.

   B. The insured pays the appropriate amount for his or her coverage.

   C. The insured does not pay his or her fair share for coverage.

   D. The insured pays a compensation fee to get into that risk pool.

2. An organization that serves as a central source of reliable information on the medical histories of insurance applicants is the

   A. American Medical Association

   B. Medical Information Bureau

   C. American College of Surgeons

   D. Government Accounting Office

3. All of the following statements about completing the application for LTC insurance are true EXCEPT

   A. any doubts an agent has about an applicant are best documented in the agent's report section of the application

   B. when an agent identifies in an applicant a condition that is deemed an unacceptable risk, the application process should cease

   C. an agent must give each applicant an outline of coverage

   D. unclear and seemingly conflicting information given by an applicant must be submitted in the application

4. According to the NAIC's guidelines for suitability, premiums should not exceed what percentage of a prospect's income?

   A. 5 percent

   B. 7 percent

   C. 9 percent

   D. 11 percent

5. According to the NAIC's guidelines for suitability, if an applicant wishes to purchase an LTC policy for asset protection, how much in assets should the applicant have?

A. $10,000

B. $20,000

C. $30,000

D. $40,000

7

Case Studies in LTC Suitability

C hapter 1 of this course went in search of a definition of suitability. Different aspects of suitability were considered, including assessing a prospect's financial status, educating a prospect so he or she can make an informed decision, identifying a prospect's needs and matching policy features and benefits to a prospect's needs. In fact, this entire text has examined these and other aspects of suitability. Now is the time to bring it all together.

An agent faces the challenge of achieving suitability every time he or she meets with a prospect. No two situations are exactly the same. This means what worked for one prospect might not work for the next. Furthermore, applying an agent's knowledge to understand a prospect's situation is a skill learned through experience.

■ ■ ■ ■ ■

■ CASE STUDIES

The four case studies this chapter contains present a variety of situations and challenges an agent typically faces when sitting across the table from a prospect for the first time. Each case study is presented in the form of a completed fact-finder for a hypothetical prospect.

An analysis of the prospect's answers to the fact-finding and feeling-finding questions follows each fact-finder. Additionally, tips advise the agent how to further educate the prospect about why long-term care insurance makes sense for him or her.

Working through these four case studies helps an agent understand the challenges in selling LTC insurance, but it won't make him or her an expert on designing LTC policies. This comes after much experience working with prospects, asking them the difficult questions they don't want to answer and listening intently to their responses. Wisdom sets in when an agent has mastered the art of designing plans most prospects want to purchase because the policies fulfill their needs.

In studying these cases, an agent should note how the completed fact-finder gives him or her clues to educating clients and guiding them in making the many decisions they face in designing suitable LTC policies. The agent should note also how often the fact-finder gives rise to further questions the agent must resolve before he or she can take an appropriate strategy in guiding clients through the maze of choices they must make in designing suitable LTC policies.

The purpose of the case studies is to show how an agent could analyze information in a fact-finder to develop a presentation and recommendations that result in a suitable sale of an LTC policy. No predetermined policy options work for these cases. Furthermore, even when an agent has a wealth of information about a prospect, no simple solution exists for the prospect's unique personal and financial situations.

As this course has indicated, designing a suitable LTC policy requires a client to make many complex decisions about care providers and settings, elimination periods, benefit amounts, benefit maximums and so forth. Guiding the client to making the best decision on each of these issues is also part of a suitable sale.

One measure of suitability is a resulting sale. A particular client purchases a policy that meets his or her needs and can pay the premiums. This means the client gets a quality product at a price that he or she can afford.

Suitability is achieved only when a client's policy performs as the client expects it to when an insurable event occurs. This final step in determining suitability is not simulated with these case studies, thus ensuring the same uncertainties agents experience when working with clients in sales situations. The first case study begins on the next page.

ILL. 7.1 ■ *Case Study #1*

Name: _David Phillips, Sr._   Spouse's Name: _Leslie Phillips_
Birthdate: _12/01/41_   Birthdate: _08/06/43_

Home Street Address: _123 W. Main Street_
City/State/Zip: _Independence, MO_

Home Phone: _____   Business Phone (W): _____
Mobile Phone: _____   Fax: _____
E-Mail Address: _____

CHILDREN

Name	Age	Lives In
David Phillips, Jr.	23	Dallas, Texas
Linda Phillips	20	St. Louis, Missouri

Do any of your children have any special needs?
David is on his own.
Linda is attending college.

Tell me about your hobbies.
play golf, volunteer at church, and garden.

Tell me about your career.
David – Worked hard as Principal of a public school. Now back in classroom.
Leslie – Works at grocery, will continue until Linda is out of school.

Why did you decide to retire? - OR- Why did you decide to continue working?
David – Not ready to retire. Still enjoys working.
Leslie – Likes the hours and pay, but no career aspirations.

ILL. 7.1 ■ *Case Study #1 (cont.)*

What are your current sources of income?

Working. In retirement it will be David's pension and well-funded 401(K).

INCOME

Wages, Salary, etc.	$ 62,500	Social Security	$
Pension Income	$	401(K) Income	$
Annuity Income	$	Investment Income	$
Trust Income	$	Other Sources	$

Total Income $ 62,500 ÷ 12 = 5,200

Do you plan to retire in your current home?

Depends on where Linda settles. May want to be near grandchildren some day.

What types of insurance do you maintain? Do you normally purchase a low or high deductible?

Health insurance through David's work. Auto, Home, Blanket Liability. Keep $1,000 deductibles.

No life insurance.

Is your Medicare-supplement plan covering all the items you expected?

N/A

LIVING EXPENSES

Mortgage/Rent	$ 400	Utilities	$ 150
Food	$ 500	Entertainment	$ 250
Insurance	$ 100	Transportation	$ 300
Vacations	$ 200	Medical Expenses	$ 50
Taxes	$ 350	Debts	$
Charities & Church	$ 250	Other Expenses	$ 1,000 (college)

Total Living Expenses $ 3,550

Total Income Less Total Expenses $ 1,650

Where have you been able to save or invest the most successfully?

David's 401(K). Also have a couple of mutual funds.

How well have you been able to diversify your retirement nest egg?

David - Pension and 401(K).

Leslie could put money in 401(K) but does not think it is necessary.

ILL. 7.1 ■ *Case Study #1 (cont.)*

Are some of your assets in tax-deferred or tax-exempt vehicles?
Yes, like tax-breaks.

SAVINGS AND INVESTMENTS

Checking Accounts	$ 2,000	Savings Accounts	$ 10,000
Certificates of Deposit	$ -	Mutual Funds	$ 75,000
Life Ins. Cash Values	$ -	Annuities	$ -
Stocks	$ -	Bonds	$ -
Real Estate	$ -	401(K)	$ 125,000
IRAs	$ 60,000 *(ISA)*	Pensions	$ -
Other Liquid Assets	$ -		

Total Savings and Investments $ 272,000

PROPERTY

Principal Residence	$ 140,000	Other Homes	$ -
Investment Property	$ -	Personal Property	$ 30,000
Valuables	$ 20,000	Vehicles	$ 32,000
Recreational Vehicles	$ -	Business Interests	$ -
Other Property	$ -		

Total Property $ 222,000

Total Assets $ 494,000

Have you been able to pay off some of your debts?
Debt-free except for mortgage.

What debts do you have outstanding?
Mortgage.

LIABILITIES

Principle Mortgage	$ 50,000 left	Home Equity Loan	$ -
Credit Cards	$ -	Installment Loans	$ -
Other Debts	$ -		

Total Liabilities $ 50,000

Net Worth   (assets minus liabilities) $ 444,000

ILL. 7.1 ■ *Case Study #1 (cont.)*

What types of legal planning have you done regarding your death or a possible illness?

Not much.

Trusts?	Yes / (No)	Will?	(Yes) / No	
Living Will?	Yes / (No)	Power of Attorney?	Yes / (No)	
Durable Power of Attorney?	Yes / (No)	Other _____		

ADVISORS

	Name	Location
Attorney	*John Phillips*	*Independence, Missouri*
Accountant	-	
Banker\Trust Officer	-	
Insurance Agent	-	
Other Advisor	-	

What experience have you had with someone needing long-term care?

David's mother needed home care for a couple of months. Leslie's father is in his 90s.
David and Leslie are nervous about the future.

What circumstances required them to need the care?

David's mother had a hip replacement a couple of years ago.

As you become old, how do you want to be cared for?

Would like to stay home, maybe have Linda help out.

Under what circumstances would you have to enter a nursing home as you age?

David Jr. and Linda live far and can't care for parents. One or both gets Alzheimer's. Don't want
to care for each other if they have Alzheimer's.

What do you know about the cost of care in the area?

David's mother had all home care covered by insurance and Medicare. Heard it is expensive.

If you had to enter a nursing home today, how would you pay for your care?

The state program. Have to use 401(K) money.

CASE STUDY #1 NEEDS ANALYSIS

David and Leslie have done an excellent job establishing a secure retirement nest egg. They have adequate income to afford LTC insurance premiums, although they are not insurance buyers. Their personal experience helps them understand the need for insurance protection, so the agent should emphasize the options available when using insurance to pay for care.

The agent needs more clarification on what the Phillips mean by "the state program" to pay for care. They likely are referring to Medicaid, so that option is easy to rule out given their assets.

David and Leslie like the idea of staying in their home to receive care. For prospects their age, having the flexibility home care coverage provides makes a lot of sense for the future. The agent's initial recommendation should include a comprehensive plan covering home and community-based care.

The daily maximum is difficult to determine given the amount of data available. The agent needs to know how David and Leslie feel about using a portion of their income to pay for long-term care. It seems as though they don't pay for much of their insurance, so providing for the full cost of care might make the most sense. This way, they won't have complaints about inadequate coverage at the time of claim. Documenting the agent's recommendation and the Phillips' final decision is essential.

The couple have adequate funds to pay the initial cost of care for many months, but not being insurance savvy, they may prefer a shorter elimination period. A thorough explanation of how the elimination period works is essential regardless of the recommendation.

This type of prospect isn't likely to want a cap on the maximum amount paid in benefits. Affordability and suitability of an unlimited maximum is not an issue; therefore, the agent should start with this option.

The issue of inflation protection probably will create a lively discussion with this couple. At their age, it is likely they'll need the protection, but affordability is an issue. The agent should stress the long-term cost-effectiveness of the 5 percent compounded annually option. Again, they might not feel that prepaying for a future benefit is important given their insurance-buying experience. If they don't purchase this option initially, the agent can stay in contact with them. When Linda graduates from college, they will be more able to afford the increased premium inherent in inflation protection.

ILL. 7.2 ■ *Case Study #2*

Name: _James O'Leary_   **Spouse's Name:** _Nancy O'Leary_

Birthdate: _4/1/30_   **Birthdate:** _6/1/28_

Home Street Address: _1721 Constitution Court_

City/State/Zip: _Boston, MA, 55555_

Home Phone: _777--555--5555_   **Business Phone (W):**

Mobile Phone: **Fax:**

E-Mail Address: _IrishPride@AOL.com_

CHILDREN

Name	Age	Lives In
Robert O'Leary	48	Manchester, New Hampshire
Bruce O'Leary	46	Concord, Massachusetts
John O'Leary	44	Boston, Massachusetts

Do any of your children have any special needs?

_No._

Tell me about your hobbies.

Travel. Prefer New York, Ireland, and St. Petersburg, Florida.

Tell me about your career.

Owned a grocery store for 40 years. Both worked there. Selling it to son John.

Why did you decide to retire? - OR- Why did you decide to continue working?

Large chain store opened nearby. Didn't want to change to a coffee shop with large bakery and deli.

ILL. 7.2 ■ *Case Study #2 (cont.)*

What are your current sources of income?

John's payments, a couple of investments and Nancy's inheritance.

INCOME

Wages, Salary, etc. $		Social Security	$ *1,500*
Pension Income $		401(K) Income	$
Annuity Income $		Investment Income $	*500*
Trust Income	$ *1,000*	Other Sources	$ *4,000* *(loan payment)*

Total Income $ *7,000*

Do you plan to retire in your current home?

Yes. Don't like Florida enough to relocate and all of the grandkids are here.

What types of insurance do you maintain? Do you normally purchase a low or high deductible?

Medicare-supplement plan F. Auto and home. Life insurance for the estate plan.
Prefer low deductibles.

Is your Medicare-supplement plan covering all the items you expected?

Would like foreign-travel coverage. Buy it now from travel agent – very expensive.

LIVING EXPENSES

Mortgage/Rent	$ *800*	Utilities	$ *400*
Food	$ *250*	Entertainment	$ *500*
Insurance	$ *1,000*	Transportation	$ *200*
Vacations	$ *-*	Medical Expenses	$ *50*
Taxes	$ *2,400*	Debts	$ *-*
Charities & Church	$ *600*	Other Expenses	$ *-*

Total Living Expenses $ *6,200*

Total Income Less Total Expenses $ *800*

Where have you been able to save or invest the most successfully?

Stock market. Invested in local companies like Wang. Fidelity funds have done well.

How well have you been able to diversify your retirement nest egg?

Good diversification. Mutual funds have helped.

ILL. 7.2 ■ *Case Study #2 (cont.)*

Are some of your assets in tax-deferred or tax-exempt vehicles?
Own a couple of annuities. Wish they had a pension or some other plan while working at store.

SAVINGS AND INVESTMENTS

Checking Accounts	$ 3,000		Savings Accounts	$ 2,000
Certificates of Deposit	$ –		Mutual Funds	$ 95,000
Life Ins. Cash Values	$ 40,000		Annuities	$ 30,000
Stocks	$ 85,000		Bonds	$ 15,000
Real Estate	$ –		401(K)	$ –
IRAs	$ –		Pensions	$ –
Other Liquid Assets	$ –			

Total Savings and Investments $ 270,000

PROPERTY

Principal Residence	$ 430,000		Other Homes	$ –
Investment Property	$ –		Personal Property	$ 60,000
Valuables	$ 18,000		Vehicles	$ 44,000
Recreational Vehicles	$ –		Business Interests	$ 300,000 *(grocery store equity.*
Other Property	$ –			*John is buying.)*

Total Property $ 852,000

Total Assets $ 1,122,000

Have you been able to pay off some of your debts?
Mortgage on the store paid off 20 years ago. Mortgage on home is very low.

What debts do you have outstanding?
Carry a little credit card debt and small mortgage.

LIABILITIES

Principle Mortgage	$ 10,000		Home Equity Loan	$ –
Credit Cards	$ 2,000		Installment Loans	$ –
Other Debts	$ –			

Total Liabilities $ 12,000

Net Worth   (assets minus liabilities) $ 1,110,000

ILL. 7.2 ■ *Case Study #2 (cont.)*

What types of legal planning have you done regarding your death or a possible illness?

Grocery store is in trust for John. Nancy's father set up a trust many years ago; eventually that money will go to boys.

Trusts?	(Yes) No	Will?	(Yes) No	
Living Will?	Yes (No)	Power of Attorney?	Yes (No)	
Durable Power of Attorney?	(Yes) No	Other	*Loan with John*	

ADVISORS

	Name	Location
Attorney	*Mike O'Conner*	*Boston*
Accountant	*Pat Mularney*	*Cambridge*
Banker\Trust Officer	*John Swanson*	*Boston*
Insurance Agent	*Kate Riley*	*Concord*
Other Advisor	–	

What experience have you had with someone needing long-term care?

Nancy's mother lived with them for 12 years before going to a nursing home for a couple of years.

What circumstances required them to need the care?

Old age and Alzheimer's. Finally a stroke put her in a home.

As you become old, how do you want to be cared for?

Prefer to stay at home. John's wife Teresa is a housewife and could help out.

Under what circumstances would you have to enter a nursing home as you age?

If completely incapacitated and needed care all the time.

What do you know about the cost of care in the area?

The homes nearby charge too much. They consider them a rip-off.

If you had to enter a nursing home today, how would you pay for your care?

Medicare. Attorney has suggested Medicaid.

CASE STUDY #2 NEEDS ANALYSIS

The O'Leary income statement shows adequate income to pay LTC insurance premiums. On top of that, they receive only about 3 percent of their investments as income. It appears the O'Learys have decided to reinvest the earnings exceeding that amount. Given that they own life insurance for estate-planning purposes, the agent could assume they believe in using insurance to shift risks.

The agent's major challenge is to help the O'Learys understand the government programs. He or she should spend some time discussing why Medicare doesn't cover much long-term care. The Medicaid issue, however, may be more difficult to communicate. With a trusted attorney encouraging them to do something other than purchase insurance, the amount of information the agent uses to support the insurance option must increase dramatically.

The prospects need to understand the limitations of Medicaid before, during and after qualifying for those benefits. Focusing on the emotional aspects of depending on Medicaid that accompany the financial qualifications can help the O'Learys see a side of this option the attorney has not discussed with them. If the O'Learys continue to insist they will depend on Medicaid to fund their long-term care, it would be prudent for the agent to investigate with a local Medicaid caseworker exactly how the store will be treated for Medicaid qualification.

Medicaid planning entails a lot of slipping through loopholes in the laws. The program's intent is to provide benefits for the poor. Unfortunately, many in the middle class think they can use this means-tested program as an entitlement program. The agent should discuss the insurance option only after receiving affirmation that the O'Learys will not dance the Medicaid two-step with their attorney.

The O'Learys stated they would prefer to receive care at home from their daughter-in-law Teresa. It would be helpful to know whether they have made plans with Teresa to provide care or whether their comments were wishful thinking. The agent should begin by recommending a comprehensive plan. Facility-only coverage might take care of their needs, but not their wants. Massachusetts regulations require the inclusion of home care benefits in all LTC plans, although facility-only coverage might be available from a carrier using creative filing techniques.

The agent should offer the O'Learys the full daily benefit. It appears a copayment type plan is viable for them; however, it's their choice.

Paying the initial cost of care to satisfy the elimination period seems affordable. While a three-month or six-month wait is possible, the O'Learys may not liquidate any investments to pay for care. With full disclosure, the agent should start with a 90-day or 100-day elimination period.

The unlimited maximum is best for the couple. An ugly situation would arise if they received their last benefit check after three years of care, then began selling assets. The ownership of the grocery store could come under scrutiny if the O'Learys considered Medicaid as a last resort. This could create ill feelings within the family if the store ended up in someone else's hands because of a long nursing home stay. The family could look to the agent for recourse if the agent recommended a shorter maximum.

Inflation protection is a good option for the O'Learys if they expect to live long lives. Affordability is always an issue, however—and especially so in this case. Most likely, the grocery store payments will end in six or seven years. Are they allowing their investments to grow so they can use more of that income later? Is it likely they'll continue to travel as much in the future? Self-insuring inflation is another option unless the couple live a long time and need a lot of care. They don't have enough assets for this option if one requires a long stay in a nursing facility. After asking the right questions, the agent should start the discussion with the long-term cost-effectiveness of the 5 percent compound option. Then the O'Learys can make the decision.

ILL. 7.3 ■ *Case Study #3*

Name: _Iris Davis_   **Spouse's Name:** _Arthur Davis (died 6 years ago)_

Birthdate: _10/14/22_   **Birthdate:** _____

Home Street Address: _4621 N. Mallard Road_ _____
City/State/Zip: _San Diego, CA 55555_ _____

Home Phone: _815-555-1212_   **Business Phone (W):** _____
Mobile Phone: _____   **Fax:** _____
E-Mail Address: _____

CHILDREN

Name	Age	Lives In
Connor Davis	_42_	_Phoenix, Arizona_
Heather Douglas	_36_	_San Diego, California_

Do any of your children have any special needs?
_No._ _____

Tell me about your hobbies.
Serves on committees at church. Helps daughter with grandchildren. Visits friends and drives them around.

Tell me about your career.
Worked at a bank until Connor was born. Art earned the money in the family.

Why did you decide to retire? - OR- Why did you decide to continue working?
Art worked too long. Wishes he would have retired sooner.

ILL. 7.3 ■ *Case Study #3 (cont.)*

What are your current sources of income?

Social Security, pension from Art's work, a few investments.

INCOME

Wages, Salary, etc.	$	Social Security	$ 1,000
Pension Income	$ 1,500	401(K) Income	$
Annuity Income	$	Investment Income	$ 200
Trust Income	$	Other Sources	$

Total Income $ 2,700

Do you plan to retire in your current home?

Plans to stay here until she dies. Has been here for 40 years, so she can't afford to move because of low taxes. Heather and her family may move in when Iris dies.

What types of insurance do you maintain? Do you normally purchase a low or high deductible?

Life insurance, home and auto; Medicare supplement; low deductibles.

Is your Medicare-supplement plan covering all the items you expected?

Yes. Has had it for more than 10 years. Blue Cross covers everything.

LIVING EXPENSES

Mortgage/Rent	$	Utilities	$ 150
Food	$ 300	Entertainment	$ 200
Insurance	$ 350	Transportation	$ 200
Vacations	$ 100	Medical Expenses	$ 100
Taxes	$ 500	Debts	$ -
Charities & Church	$ 200	Other Expenses	$

Total Living Expenses $ 2,100

Total Income Less Total Expenses $ 600

Where have you been able to save or invest the most successfully?

Does not have much savings.

How well have you been able to diversify your retirement nest egg?

Not very well.

ILL. 7.3 ■ *Case Study #3 (cont.)*

Are some of your assets in tax-deferred or tax-exempt vehicles?

No.

SAVINGS AND INVESTMENTS

Checking Accounts	$ *5,000*	Savings Accounts	$ *5,000*
Certificates of Deposit	$ *20,000*	Mutual Funds	$ *10,000*
Life Ins. Cash Values	$ *5,000*	Annuities	$ *-*
Stocks	$ *-*	Bonds	$ *-*
Real Estate	$ *-*	401(K)	$ *-*
IRAs	$ *25,000*	Pensions	$ *-*
Other Liquid Assets	$ *-*		

Total Savings and Investments $ *70,000*

PROPERTY

Principal Residence	$ *350,000*	Other Homes	$ *-*
Investment Property	$ *-*	Personal Property	$ *10,000*
Valuables	$ *40,000*	Vehicles	$ *20,000*
Recreational Vehicles	$ *-*	Business Interests	$ *-*
Other Property	$ *-*		

Total Property $ *420,000*

Total Assets $ *490,000*

Have you been able to pay off some of your debts?

All of them.

What debts do you have outstanding?

None.

LIABILITIES

Principle Mortgage	$	Home Equity Loan	$
Credit Cards	$	Installment Loans	$
Other Debts	$		

Total Liabilities $

Net Worth (assets minus liabilities) $ *490,000*

ILL. 7.3 ■ *Case Study #3 (cont.)*

What types of legal planning have you done regarding your death or a possible illness?

Just a will.

Trusts?	Yes / (No)	Will?	(Yes) / No
Living Will?	Yes / (No)	Power of Attorney?	Yes / (No)
Durable Power of Attorney?	Yes / (No)	Other	

ADVISORS

	Name	Location
Attorney	*William Stone*	*San Diego*
Accountant	-	
Banker\Trust Officer	-	
Insurance Agent	-	
Other Advisor	-	

What experience have you had with someone needing long-term care?

Husband was sick for a couple of months at home.

What circumstances required them to need the care?

Stroke. Never got better.

As you become old, how do you want to be cared for?

Wants her daughter to care for her. If it gets too much, Shady Oaks has a nice facility.

Under what circumstances would you have to enter a nursing home as you age?

Becomes too much of a burden on her daughter Heather.

What do you know about the cost of care in the area?

It's very expensive.

If you had to enter a nursing home today, how would you pay for your care?

No idea – maybe use the IRA or mutual fund.

CASE STUDY #3 NEEDS ANALYSIS

This widow has the vast majority of her assets in her home. Although modest in size, it has appreciated significantly over the years. It is well maintained, is built on one level (ranch home) and has good access to services. Her daughter lives nearby and is willing and able to provide care.

Iris has excess income, so affordability for a basic plan isn't an issue. Using the IRA or mutual fund income is an alternative to using current income to pay the premiums because she thinks that is where she will get the money to pay for care.

Iris's pride is wrapped up in passing her home to Heather and her family. As a widow, she will have difficulty protecting the home from Medi-Cal (Medicaid in California). The ability to choose a good facility is also important to Iris. Her limited liquid assets may make it more difficult to get in one of the better facilities in the area, however.

Iris wants to stay in her home to receive care. She doesn't want to overburden Heather, though, so going to a facility is a realistic alternative. In this case, the agent should propose a comprehensive plan. The fallback would be facility-only coverage.

Shady Oaks currently charges $175 per day, and Iris likes low deductibles. She could use some of her excess income plus some of her normal living expenses to offset the full cost of care in the facility. And remember, her waiver of premium kicks in while she is in the facility, so she can use the outlay committed to paying the premiums to reduce the daily benefit needed. This reduction in coverage may make the home care coverage more affordable.

Given Iris's limited cash on hand, a shorter elimination period is appropriate. The longest period should be 90 or 100 days. At today's cost of care, that would use all of the IRA and a chunk of the mutual fund to pay the initial cost of care until the elimination period is satisfied. An elimination period of 10, 20 or 30 days might be a better option.

If Iris is concerned about passing her home to Heather, the unlimited maximum is her best bet to ensure that the home isn't liquidated to pay for care if she stays a long while in a nursing facility. The unlimited plan may stretch her budget too far, however, perhaps her children are willing and able to pay the difference in the premium between an unlimited maximum and a three-year maximum.

The need for inflation protection lessens as people age. Because Iris is 78 years old, the cost does not add as much to the premium as it would for someone in his or her 50s. The agent is required, by law, to offer the inflation protection. Iris's decision depends on how long she thinks she'll live. If she expects to live into her 90s, adding inflation protection is the most cost-effective way to keep her coverage up to date. This may be another portion of the premium her children wish to pay.

ILL. 7.4 ■ *Case Study #4*

Name: *Gerhard Schmitt* **Spouse's Name:** *Hildegard Schmitt*

Birthdate: *1/14/35* **Birthdate:** *3/1/35*

Home Street Address: *1535 E. Wisconsin Ave.*

City/State/Zip: *Milwaukee, WI.*

Home Phone: *414-555-1212* **Business Phone (W):**

Mobile Phone: **Fax:**

E-Mail Address:

CHILDREN

Name	Age	Lives In
Johann Schmitt	*47*	*Germantown, Wisconsin*
Maria Mueller	*45*	*Madison, Wisconsin*
Joseph Schmitt	*44*	*Green Bay, Wisconsin*
Anna Knarr	*42*	*Chicago, Illinois*

Do any of your children have any special needs?

Maria has MS, but is independent and raising a family.

Tell me about your hobbies.

Playing cards at the German Club, vegetable gardening, and visiting their lake cottage up north.

Tell me about your career.

Gerhard worked in the same mill his entire life, was union steward and secretary. For fun and a little extra money, they transport cars to a local dealer.

Why did you decide to retire? - OR- Why did you decide to continue working?

Mill shut down two years ago, so he took early retirement.

ILL. 7.4 ■ *Case Study #4 (cont.)*

What are your current sources of income?

Pension and Social Security.

INCOME

Wages, Salary, etc.	$ 500	Social Security	$ 1,800
Pension Income	$ 3,100	401(K) Income	$
Annuity Income	$	Investment Income	$
Trust Income	$	Other Sources	$

Total Income $ 5,400

Do you plan to retire in your current home?

It's paid for, so why move?

What types of insurance do you maintain? Do you normally purchase a low or high deductible?

Auto and home. The union provides everything else.

Is your Medicare-supplement plan covering all the items you expected?

Adequate, but they're concerned about prescription coverage.

LIVING EXPENSES

Mortgage/Rent	$	Utilities	$ 350
Food	$ 400	Entertainment	$ 400
Insurance	$ 150	Transportation	$ 200
Vacations	$ 300	Medical Expenses	$ 600
Taxes	$ 200	Debts	$
Charities & Church	$ 1,000	Other Expenses	$ 200 (cottage loan)

Total Living Expenses $ 3,800

Total Income Less Total Expenses $ 1,600

Where have you been able to save or invest the most successfully?

CDs at the bank and company stock.

How well have you been able to diversify your retirement nest egg?

Don't like risky investments like mutual funds.

ILL. 7.4 ■ *Case Study #4 (cont.)*

Are some of your assets in tax-deferred or tax-exempt vehicles?

No. (comment – he actually has an IRA)

SAVINGS AND INVESTMENTS

Checking Accounts	$ *1,500*	Savings Accounts	$ *10,000*
Certificates of Deposit	$ *60,000*	Mutual Funds	$ *–*
Life Ins. Cash Values	$ *–*	Annuities	$ *–*
Stocks	$ *15,000*	Bonds	$ *–*
Real Estate	$ *–*	401(K)	$ *–*
IRAs	$ *8,000*	Pensions	$ *–*
Other Liquid Assets	$ *–*		

Total Savings and Investments $ *94,500*

PROPERTY

Principal Residence	$ *110,000*	Other Homes	$ *–*
Investment Property	$ *60,000*	Personal Property	$ *20,000*
Valuables	$ *8,000 (hummel collect.)*	Vehicles	$ *12,000*
Recreational Vehicles	$ *–*	Business Interests	$ *–*
Other Property	$ *–*		

Total Property $ *210,000*

Total Assets $ *304,500*

Have you been able to pay off some of your debts?

Paid off mortgage last year. Never used credit cards.

What debts do you have outstanding?

Mortgage on lake cottage.

LIABILITIES

Principle Mortgage	$	Home Equity Loan	$
Credit Cards	$	Installment Loans	$
Other Debts	$ *20,000*		

Total Liabilities $ *20,000*

Net Worth   (assets minus liabilities) $ *284,500*

ILL. 7.4 ■ *Case Study #4 (cont.)*

What types of legal planning have you done regarding your death or a possible illness?

None.

Trusts?	Yes / (No)	Will?	Yes / (No)
Living Will?	Yes / (No)	Power of Attorney?	Yes / (No)
Durable Power of Attorney?	Yes / (No)	Other	

ADVISORS

	Name	Location
Attorney	_____	_____
Accountant	_____	_____
Banker\Trust Officer	_____	_____
Insurance Agent	_____	_____
Other Advisor	_____	_____

What experience have you had with someone needing long-term care?

When Hildegard was growing up, her grandparents lived with her family for 8 years. Marie needed extra care when diagnosed with MS. She is doing much better now.

What circumstances required them to need the care?

Grandparents got old.

As you become old, how do you want to be cared for?

Want the kids to take care of them.

Under what circumstances would you have to enter a nursing home as you age?

Gerhard – Rather be dead than in a nursing home.

Hildegard – Kids unable to care for her. Husband won't do it.

What do you know about the cost of care in the area?

Can't be too much. A lot of people live in those homes.

If you had to enter a nursing home today, how would you pay for your care?

Government will take care of them.

CASE STUDY #4 NEEDS ANALYSIS

This difficult case will take time to close. Given the fact the Schmitts were willing to meet with the agent and complete the fact-finder is reason for hope.

The agent can use the three rings in Illustration 3.3 (page 35) to explain how care from the family is supplemented with community and professional services. Furthermore, all of the Schmitt's children except Johann live a couple of hours away from them. A "willing and able" discussion may help Gerhard understand that relying on family isn't as easy as it was 30 years ago.

The agent might want to probe more deeply in determining the Schmitt's personal experience with long-term care. Few people in retirement today don't have a friend, a neighbor or an acquaintance who needed care at some time. Helping Maria through her challenges with multiple sclerosis should help the couple understand the burden of caring for someone.

It appears as though affordability isn't a problem, but a big chasm lies between having the money and parting with it. Spending extra time with the Schmitts can help the agent bring them around, and asking lots of questions can help them understand how they will benefit from owning LTC coverage.

The couple's lack of understanding about the cost of care is troubling. Their most recent experience of a loved one needing care was probably 50 years ago. The agent should provide them with a survey of the various providers in the area.

The agent should not discuss the product until both Gerhard and Hildegard agree that insurance is the right way to go. Then the agent should have a good idea of where the premium dollars will come from. Sure there is plenty of income in the analysis, but most likely the Schmitts are not ready to spend it on insurance. They've never really paid much for insurance in the past.

Insurability is an issue, so the agent needs to know more about Gerhard's prescriptions.

Designing a product for the Schmitts is a challenge. They probably will prefer modest coverage rather than a full-blown plan. This is a case where facility-only coverage makes the most sense. Realistically, the kids are not available to help out because of distance, and Gerhard isn't likely to care for his wife. The agent needs to ask a few more questions before making a final recommendation here, however.

The agent should start with the daily benefit at the full cost of care, especially if the focus is on facility-only coverage. If the Schmitts choose anything less than full cost of care, the kids will wonder why it wasn't included when they file a claim. The same goes for the elimination period. The agent should recommend a short one for the benefit of the persons filing the claim. First impressions at claim time are important in this case. Furthermore, the Schmitts don't have a lot of cash to pay the initial cost of care.

The most flexibility lies in the benefit maximum. The agent should find out when the Schmitts want their last check. A three-year maximum likely will satisfy them.

The inflation protection is a tough call. Yes, they're at an age where it makes sense. They're likely to own the coverage for at least 15 years, which would erode this policy's purchasing power significantly without the inflation feature. If the recommendation is for facility-only coverage with a three-year maximum, adding the 5 percent compounded inflation option makes sense. Adding it to a comprehensive plan with an unlimited maximum may stretch the Schmitt's budget too far. The agent can stress the benefit of owning the inflation option by showing the couple the future daily benefit maximum and its long-term cost-effectiveness.

■ SUMMARY

Designing a suitable LTC policy requires a client to make many complex decisions about care providers and settings, elimination periods, benefit amounts, benefit maximums and so forth. Completed fact-finders give agents clues on how to educate clients and advise them in making these many decisions in designing suitable policies. When a client purchases a policy that meets his or her needs and can afford the premiums, a suitable sale has been made. Ultimately, however, a suitable sale is demonstrated only when an insurable event occurs and the policy performs as the client expects it to.

■ CHAPTER 7 QUESTIONS FOR REVIEW

1. Understanding a prospect's family situation helps an agent

   A. eliminate the Medicaid objection

   B. design an appropriate plan

   C. eliminate the Medicare objection

   D. do all of the above

2. The appropriate benefit maximum is determined by

   A. the affordability of the premiums

   B. the benefits Medicare provides

   C. state insurance department regulations

   D. the availability of children to provide care

3. Every prospect is best served by

   A. standardized contract language

   B. a predetermined daily benefit, elimination period, benefit maximum and inflation option

   C. a careful analysis of the prospect's financial and personal situations

   D. a comprehensive policy covering as many benefits as possible

4. A suitable sale is one in which the

   A. policy meets the client's needs and is affordable

   B. policy performs as expected at claim time

   C. client makes many decisions after careful analysis

   D. all of the above

5. Which of the following statements is true of a completed fact-finder?

   A. It provides all of the information necessary to make a sale.

   B. It can be finished by the prospect before meeting with the agent.

   C. It gives the agent clues on how to work with the prospect in designing a suitable policy.

   D. It must be submitted with the application before underwriting can begin.

...... Answer Key to Questions for Review

Chapter 1

1. A
2. D
3. B
4. C
5. A

Chapter 2

1. C
2. C
3. B
4. C
5. B

Chapter 3

1. C
2. A
3. B
4. B
5. A

Chapter 4

1. C
2. B
3. A
4. C
5. C

Chapter 5

1. A
2. C
3. D
4. A
5. A

Chapter 6

1. C
2. B
3. D
4. B
5. C

Chapter 7

1. B
2. A
3. C
4. D
5. C

.....

Appendix A
LTC Insurance Personal
Worksheet

Long Term Care Insurance
Personal Worksheet

People buy long-term care insurance for many reasons. Some don't want to use their own assets to pay for long-term care. Some buy insurance to make sure they can choose the type of care they get. Others don't want their family to have to pay for care or don't want to go on Medicaid. But long term care insurance may be expensive, and may not be right for everyone.

By state law, the insurance company must **ask** you to fill out this worksheet to help you and the company decide if you should buy this policy.

Premium

The premium for the coverage you are thinking about buying will be [$_____ per month, or $_____ per year,] [a one-time single premium of $_____.]

[The company cannot raise your rates on this policy.] [The company has a right to increase premiums in the future.] The company has sold long-term care insurance since [year] and has sold this policy since [year]. [The last rate increase for this policy in this state was in [year], when premiums went up by an average of _____%]. [The company has not raised its rates for this policy.]

Drafting Note: The issuer shall use the bracketed sentence or sentences applicable to the product offered. If a company includes a statement regarding not having raised rates, it must disclose the company's rate increases under prior policies providing essentially similar coverage. The issuer may include rate information for up to two policy forms if the issuer has not changed rates on either policy form or for prior policies providing essentially similar coverage.

[☐ Have you considered whether you could afford to keep this policy if the premiums went up, for example, by 20%?]

Drafting Note: The issuer shall use the bracketed sentence unless the policy is fully paid up or is a noncancellable policy.

How will you pay each year's premium?
☐From my Income   ☐From my Savings\Investments   ☐My Family will pay

Income

What is your annual income? (check one)
☐Under $10,000   ☐$[10-20,000]   ☐$[20-30,000]   ☐$[30-50,000]   ☐Over $50,000

Drafting Note: The issuer may choose the numbers to put in the brackets to fit its suitability standards.

How do you expect your income to change over the next 10 years? (check one)
☐No change   ☐Increase   ☐Decrease

If you will be paying premiums from your own income, a rule of thumb is that you may not be able to afford this policy if the premiums will be more than 7% of your income.

Turn the Page

Savings and Investments

Not counting your home, about how much are all of your assets worth (your savings and investments)? (check one)

☐Under $20,000 ☐$20,000-$30,000 ☐$30,000-$50,000 ☐Over $50,000

How do you expect your assets to change over the next ten years? (check one)
☐Stay about the same ☐Increase ☐Decrease

If you are buying this policy to protect your assets and your assets are less than $30,000, you may wish to consider other options for financing your long-term care.

Disclosure Statement

☐	The answers to the questions above describe my financial situation.	☐	I choose not to complete this information.

Signed: _____   _____
    (Applicant)   (Date)

[☐ I explained to the applicant the importance of completing this information.

Signed: _____   _____
    (Agent)   (Date)

Agent's Printed Name: _____]

[**Note:** In order for us to process your application, please return this signed statement to [name of company], along with your application.]

[My agent has advised me that this policy does not seem to be suitable for me. However, I still want the company to consider my application.

Signed: _____   _____]
    (Applicant)   (Date)

Drafting Note: Choose the appropriate sentences depending on whether this is a direct mail or agent sale.

The company may contact you to verify your answers.

Drafting Note: When the Long-Term Care Insurance Personal Worksheet is furnished to employees and their spouses under employer group policies, the text from the heading "Disclosure Statement" to the end of the page may be removed.

Appendix B
Things to Know Before You Buy LTC Insurance

Things You Should Know Before You Buy
Long-Term Care Insurance

Long-Term Care Insurance	• A long-term care insurance policy may pay most of the costs for your care in a nursing home. Many policies also pay for care at home or other community settings. Since policies can vary in coverage, you should read this policy and make sure you understand what it covers before you buy it.
	• [You should **not** buy this insurance policy unless you can afford to pay the premiums every year.] [Remember that the company can increase premiums in the future.]

Drafting Note: For single premium policies, delete this bullet; for noncancellable policies, delete the second sentence only.

	• The personal worksheet includes questions designed to help you and the company determine whether this policy is suitable for your needs.
Medicare	• Medicare does **not** pay for most long-term care.
Medicaid	• Medicaid will generally pay for long-term care if you have very little income and few assets. You probably should **not** buy this policy if you are now eligible for Medicaid.
	• Many people become eligible for Medicaid after they have used up their own financial resources by paying for long-term care services.
	• When Medicaid pays your spouse's nursing home bills, you are allowed to keep your house and furniture, a living allowance, and some of your joint assets.
	• Your choice of long-term care services may be limited if you are receiving Medicaid. To learn more about Medicaid, contact your local or state Medicaid agency.
Shopper's Guide	• Make sure the insurance company or agent gives you a copy of a book called the National Association of Insurance Commissioners' "Shopper's Guide to Long-Term Care Insurance." Read it carefully. If you have decided to apply for long-term care insurance, you have the right to return the policy within 30 days and get back any premium you have paid if you are dissatisfied for any reason or choose not to purchase the policy.
Counseling	• Free counseling and additional information about long-term care insurance are available through your state's insurance counseling program. Contact your state insurance department or department on aging for more information about the senior health insurance counseling program in your state.

Long-Term Care Insurance Suitability Letter

Dear [Applicant]:

Your recent application for long-term care insurance included a "personal worksheet," which asked questions about your finances and your reasons for buying long-term care insurance. For your protection, state law requires us to consider this information when we review your application, to avoid selling a policy to those who may not need coverage.

[Your answers indicate that long-term care insurance may not meet your financial needs. We suggest that you review the information provided along with your application, including the booklet "Shopper's Guide to Long-Term Care Insurance" and the page titled "Things You Should Know Before Buying Long-Term Care Insurance." Your state insurance department also has information about long-term care insurance and may be able to refer you to a counselor free of charge who can help you decide whether to buy this policy.]

[You chose not to provide any financial information for us to review.]

Drafting Note: Choose the paragraph that applies.

We have suspended our final review of your application. If, after careful consideration, you still believe this policy is what you want, check the appropriate box below and return this letter to us within the next 60 days. We will then continue reviewing your application and issue a policy if you meet our medical standards.

If we do not hear from you within the next 60 days, we will close your file and not issue you a policy. You should understand that you will not have any coverage until we hear back from you, approve your application and issue you a policy.

Please check one box and return in the enclosed envelope.

☐   **Yes,** [although my worksheet indicates that long-term care insurance may not be a suitable purchase,] I wish to purchase this coverage. Please resume review of my application.

Drafting Note: Delete the phrase in brackets if the applicant did not answer the questions about income.

☐   **No.** I have decided not to buy a policy at this time.

_____   _____
APPLICANT'S SIGNATURE   DATE

Please return to [issuer] at [address] by [date].

Appendix C
1999 Form 8853
and Instructions

Form **8853**	**Medical Savings Accounts** **and Long-Term Care Insurance Contracts**	OMB No. 1545-1561
Department of the Treasury Internal Revenue Service	▶ **Attach to Form 1040.** ▶ **See separate instructions.**	19**99** Attachment Sequence No. **39**

Name(s) shown on return	Social security number of MSA account holder. If both spouses have MSAs, see page 1 ▶

Section A. Medical Savings Accounts (MSAs).

If you only have a Medicare+Choice MSA, skip Section A and complete Section B.

General Information. You MUST complete this part if you (or your spouse, if married filing jointly) established a new MSA for 1999 (even if the contributions to the MSA were made by an employer).

			Yes	No
1a	Did you establish a new MSA for 1999?	1a		
b	If "Yes," were you a previously uninsured account holder (see page 2 of the instructions for definition)?	1b		
c	If line 1a is "Yes," indicate coverage under high deductible health plan: ☐ Self-Only **or** ☐ Family			
2a	If you were married, did your spouse establish a new MSA for 1999?	2a		
b	If "Yes," was your spouse a previously uninsured account holder (see page 2 of the instructions)?	2b		
c	If line 2a is "Yes," indicate coverage under high deductible health plan: ☐ Self-Only **or** ☐ Family			

MSA Contributions and Deductions. See page 2 of the instructions before completing this part.
If you and your spouse each have high deductible health plans with self-only coverage, check here ▶ ☐
If you check this box, complete a separate Part II for each spouse (see page 2 of the instructions).

3a	Were any employer contributions made to your MSA(s)? ☐ **Yes** ☐ **No**		
b	Enter all employer contributions to your MSA(s) for 1999 ▶		
4	Enter MSA contributions that you made for 1999, including those made from January 1, 2000, through April 17, 2000, that were for 1999. Do not include rollovers (see page 2 of the instructions)	**4**	
5	Enter your limitation from the worksheet on page 3 of the instructions	**5**	
6	Enter your compensation (see page 2 of the instructions) from the employer maintaining the high deductible health plan. If you (and your spouse, if married filing jointly) have more than one plan, see **How To Complete Part II** on page 2 of the instructions. (If self-employed, enter your earned income from the trade or business under which the high deductible health plan was established.)	**6**	
7	**MSA deduction.** Enter the **smallest** of line 4, 5, or 6 here and on Form 1040, line 25	**7**	

Note: If line 4 is more than line 7, you may have to pay an additional tax. See page 3 of the instructions for details.

MSA Distributions

8a	Enter the total MSA distributions you and your spouse received from all MSAs during 1999 (see page 4 of the instructions)	**8a**	
b	Enter any distributions included on line 8a that you rolled over to another MSA (see page 4 of the instructions). Also include any excess contributions (and the earnings on those excess contributions) included on line 8a that were withdrawn by the due date of your return	**8b**	
c	Subtract line 8b from line 8a	**8c**	
9	Enter your total unreimbursed qualified medical expenses (see page 4 of the instructions)	**9**	
10	**Taxable MSA distributions.** Subtract line 9 from line 8c. If zero or less, enter -0-. Also include this amount in the total on Form 1040, line 21. On the dotted line next to line 21, enter "MSA" and show the amount	**10**	
11a	If you meet any of the **Exceptions to the 15% Tax** (see page 4 of the instructions), check ▶ ☐		
b	If you do not meet any of the exceptions, enter 15% (.15) of line 10 here and also include it in the total on Form 1040, line 56. On the dotted line next to line 56, enter "MSA" and the amount	**11b**	

Section B. Medicare+Choice MSA Distributions.

If you are married filing jointly and both you and your spouse received distributions from a Medicare+Choice MSA in 1999, complete a separate Section B for each spouse. See page 4 of the instructions.

12	Enter the total distributions you received from all Medicare+Choice MSAs in 1999	**12**	
13	Enter your total unreimbursed qualified medical expenses (see page 5 of the instructions)	**13**	
14	**Taxable Medicare+Choice MSA Distributions.** Subtract line 13 from line 12. If zero or less, enter -0-. Also include this amount in the total on Form 1040, line 21. On the dotted line next to line 21, enter "Med+MSA" and show the amount	**14**	
15a	If you meet any of the **Exceptions to the 50% Tax** (see page 5 of the instructions), check ▶ ☐		
b	If you do not meet any of the exceptions, enter 50% (.5) of line 14 here and include it in the total on Form 1040, line 56. On the dotted line next to line 56, enter "Med+MSA" and the amount	**15b**	

For Paperwork Reduction Act Notice, see page 8 of the instructions.   Cat. No. 24091H   Form **8853** (1999)

Name of policyholder (as shown on Form 1040)	Social security number of policyholder ▶

Section C. Long-Term Care (LTC) Insurance Contracts.
See **Filing Requirements for Section C** on page 6 of the instructions before completing this section.

If more than one Section C is attached, check here . . . . ▶ ☐

16a Name of insured ▶ _____ **b** Social security number of insured ▶ _____

17 In 1999, did anyone other than you receive payments on a per diem or other periodic basis under a qualified LTC insurance contract covering the insured, or receive accelerated death benefits under a life insurance policy covering the insured? . . . . ☐ Yes　☐ No

18 Was the insured a terminally ill individual? . . . . ☐ Yes　☐ No

Note: *If "Yes" and the **only** payments you received in 1999 were accelerated death benefits that were paid to you because the insured was terminally ill, skip lines 19 through 27 and enter -0- on line 28.*

19 Gross LTC payments received on a per diem or other periodic basis. Enter the total of the amounts from box 1 of all Forms 1099-LTC you received with respect to the insured on which the "Per diem" box in box 3 is checked **19**

Caution: *Do **not** use lines 20 through 28 to figure the taxable amount of benefits paid under an LTC insurance contract that is not a **qualified** LTC insurance contract. Instead, if the benefits are not excludable from your income (for example, if the benefits are not paid for personal injuries or sickness through accident or health insurance), report the amount not excludable as income on Form 1040, line 21.*

20 Enter the part of the amount on line 19 that is from **qualified** LTC insurance contracts . . . **20**

21 Accelerated death benefits received on a per diem or other periodic basis. Do not include any amounts you received because the insured was terminally ill. See page 5 of the instructions . **21**

22 Add lines 20 and 21 . . . . **22**

Note: *If you checked "Yes" on line 17 above, see the instructions for line 17 on page 5 before completing lines 23 through 27.*

23 Multiply $190 by the number of days in the LTC period **23**

24 Enter the costs incurred for qualified LTC services provided for the insured during the LTC period (see page 6 of the instructions). . . **24**

25 Enter the **larger** of line 23 or line 24 . . . . **25**

26 Enter the total reimbursements received for qualified LTC services provided for the insured during the LTC period **26**

Caution: *If you received any reimbursements from LTC contracts issued before August 1, 1996, see page 7 of the instructions.*

27 Per diem limitation. Subtract line 26 from line 25 . . . . **27**

28 **Taxable payments.** Subtract line 27 from line 22. If zero or less, enter -0-. Also include this amount in the total on Form 1040, line 21. On the dotted line next to line 21, enter "LTC" and the amount **28**

Form **8853** (1999)

1999

Instructions for Form 8853

Medical Savings Accounts and Long-Term Care Insurance Contracts

Section references are to the Internal Revenue Code unless otherwise noted.

General Instructions

A Change To Note

Use new Section B to report distributions from a Medicare+Choice medical savings account (MSA).

Purpose of Form

Use Form 8853 to:

- Report information about MSAs (other than Medicare+Choice MSAs) established in 1999;
- Report MSA contributions;
- Figure your MSA deduction;
- Report distributions from MSAs or Medicare+Choice MSAs;
- Report taxable payments from long-term care (LTC) insurance contracts; or
- Report taxable accelerated death benefits from a life insurance policy.

   Additional information. See Pub. 969, Medical Savings Accounts, for more details on MSAs.

Who Must File

You **MUST** file Form 8853 if any of the following apply.

- You (or your spouse, if married filing jointly) established a new MSA for 1999 (even if the contributions to the MSA were made by an employer).
- An employer or you (or your spouse, if married filing jointly) made contributions for 1999 to your MSA (or your spouse's MSA, if married filing jointly).
- You (or your spouse, if married filing jointly) received MSA or Medicare+Choice MSA distributions in 1999.
- You acquired an interest in an MSA or a Medicare+Choice MSA because of the death of the account holder. See **Death of Account Holder** on page 4 or 5 for details.
- You (or your spouse, if married filing jointly) were a policyholder who received payments under an LTC insurance contract, or received any accelerated death benefits from a life insurance policy, on a per diem or other periodic basis, in 1999. See the instructions for Section C, beginning on page 5.

Specific Instructions

Name and Social Security Number (SSN). Enter your name(s) and SSN as shown on your tax return. If married filing jointly and both you and your spouse each have an MSA or each have a Medicare+Choice MSA, enter the SSN shown first on your tax return.

Section A—Medical Savings Accounts (MSAs)

Eligible Individual

To be eligible for an MSA, you must be an employee of a small employer or be self-employed. You must also have a high deductible health plan (HDHP), and have no other health insurance coverage except permitted coverage. You must be an eligible individual on the first day of a month to take an MSA deduction for that month.

Small Employer

A small employer is generally an employer who had an average of 50 or fewer employees during either of the last 2 calendar years. See Pub. 969 for details.

Medical Savings Account

An MSA is an account set up exclusively for paying the qualified medical expenses of the account holder or the account holder's spouse or dependent(s) in conjunction with an HDHP.

Qualified Medical Expenses

Generally, qualified medical expenses for MSA purposes are unreimbursed medical expenses that could otherwise be deducted on Schedule A (Form 1040). See the Schedule A (Form 1040) instructions and **Pub. 502,** Medical and Dental Expenses. However, you **cannot** treat insurance premiums as qualified medical expenses, **unless** the premiums are for:

- Long-term care (LTC) insurance,
- Health care continuation coverage, or
- Health care coverage while receiving unemployment compensation under Federal or state law.

High Deductible Health Plan (HDHP)

An HDHP is a health plan that meets the following requirements:

	Self-only coverage	Family coverage
Minimum annual deductible	$1,550	$3,050
Maximum annual deductible	$2,300	$4,600
Maximum annual out-of-pocket expenses	$3,050	$5,600

Other Health Insurance

If you have an MSA, you (and your spouse, if you have family coverage) may not have any other health insurance coverage (other than an HDHP).

Exception. You may have additional insurance that provides benefits only for:

   1. Accidents,
   2. Disability,
   3. Dental care,
   4. Vision care,
   5. Long-term care,
   6. Liabilities under workers' compensation laws, tort liabilities, or liabilities arising from the ownership or use of property,
   7. A specific disease or illness, or
   8. A fixed amount per day (or other period) of hospitalization.

Disabled

An individual is generally considered disabled if he or she is unable to engage in any substantial gainful activity due to a physical or mental impairment which can be expected to result in death or to continue indefinitely.

Part I—General Information

Complete this part if you (or your spouse, if married filing jointly) established a new MSA for 1999, even if the contributions to the MSA were made by an employer.

Lines 1a and 2a

Check "Yes" if you or your spouse established a new MSA for 1999, including an MSA established for 1999 from January 1, 2000, through April 17, 2000.

Lines 1b and 2b

Previously Uninsured Account Holder

If an account holder has **self-only coverage** under an HDHP and did not have any health plan coverage at any time during the 6-month period before coverage under the HDHP began, the account holder is considered previously uninsured. In addition, for the account holder to be considered previously uninsured, the HDHP coverage must not have begun before July 1, 1996.

If an account holder has **family coverage** under an HDHP and neither the account holder nor the account holder's spouse had any health plan coverage at any time during the 6-month period before coverage under the HDHP began, the account holder is considered previously uninsured. In addition, for the account holder to be considered previously uninsured, the HDHP coverage must not have begun before July 1, 1996.

In determining whether an account holder is previously uninsured, disregard any health insurance that is permitted in addition to the HDHP. See **Other Health Insurance** on page 1.

Line 1c

If you were covered by an HDHP with self-only coverage and an HDHP with family coverage, indicate which plan was in effect longer during the year.

Line 2c

If you are filing a joint return and your spouse was covered by an HDHP with self-only coverage and an HDHP with family coverage, indicate which plan was in effect longer during the year.

Part II—MSA Contributions and Deductions

Use Part II to figure:

1. Your MSA deduction (and, if applicable, any excess contributions you made); and

2. Any excess contributions made by an employer. See **Excess Employer Contributions** on page 3.

Figuring Your MSA Deduction

The amount you can deduct for MSA contributions is limited by:

1. The applicable portion of the policy's annual deductible (line 5), and

2. Your compensation from the employer maintaining the HDHP (line 6).

However, employer contributions to an MSA may prevent you from making deductible contributions. In addition, if you or your spouse made contributions in addition to any employer contributions, you may have to pay an additional tax

(see **Excess Contributions You Make** on page 3 for details).

Employer Contributions to an MSA

The following rules apply for employer contributions.

1. If an employer made contributions to your MSA, you are not entitled to a deduction.

2. If you and your spouse are covered under an HDHP with family coverage, employer contributions to either of your MSAs prevent either spouse from making deductible contributions to an MSA.

3. If you and your spouse each have MSAs with self-only coverage and one of you received employer contributions to his or her MSA, the other is allowed to make deductible contributions to an MSA.

The following examples illustrate these rules:

Example 1. Your employer maintains an HDHP with family coverage. Your employer does not contribute to your MSA. However, your spouse (who is covered under the HDHP maintained by your employer) has an employer that contributes to his or her MSA. You are not allowed to deduct contributions to your MSA because of the employer contribution to your spouse's MSA.

Example 2. Your employer maintains an HDHP with self-only coverage. Your spouse's employer maintains an HDHP with self-only coverage. Your employer contributes to your MSA. No employer contributions are made to your spouse's MSA. Your spouse may deduct contributions to his or her MSA.

How To Complete Part II

Complete lines 3a through 7 as instructed on the form unless one of the following applies.

1. If employer contributions to an MSA prevent you from taking a deduction for amounts you contributed to your MSA, complete Part II as follows:

   a. Complete lines 3a through 4.

   b. Skip lines 5 and 6.

   c. Enter -0- on line 7.

   d. If line 4 is more than zero, see **Excess Contributions You Make** and **Excess Employer Contributions** on page 3.

2. If you and your spouse have more than one MSA, complete lines 3a through 7 as follows:

• If either spouse has an HDHP with family coverage, complete lines 3a through 7 using the **Family Coverage** rules in the instructions for line 5.

• If both spouses have HDHPs with self-only coverage, check the box in the heading for Part II. Complete a separate Form 8853, Section A, Part II, for each spouse. Write "statement" across the top, fill in the name and SSN and complete

Part II. Then, add the totals for lines 3b, 4, and 7 from the two separate statement Forms 8853 and enter those totals on the respective lines of the controlling Form 8853 (the combined Form 8853 for both spouses). Do not complete lines 3a, 5, and 6 of the controlling Form 8853. Attach the two statement Forms 8853 to the controlling Form 8853.

Lines 3a and 3b

Employer Contributions

Employer contributions include any amount an employer contributes to any MSA for you or your spouse for 1999. These contributions should be shown in box 13 of Form W-2 with code R. See **Excess Employer Contributions** on page 3 for details.

Line 4

Do not include amounts rolled over from another MSA. See **Rollovers** on page 4.

Line 5

Use the worksheet on page 3 to figure your limitation.

Instructions for Line 5 Limitation Worksheet

Go through the chart for each month of 1999. Enter the result on the corresponding line next to the month on the worksheet.

 If your eligibility and coverage did not change from one month to the next, enter the same number you entered for the previous month.

More than one HDHP. If you (and your spouse, if married filing jointly) had more than one HDHP on the first of the month and one of the plans has family coverage, use the **Family Coverage** rules below and disregard any plans with self-only coverage.

   Self-Only Coverage. Enter the annual deductible, which must be at least $1,550 but not more than $2,300. Enter 65% (.65) of the annual deductible on the worksheet.

   Family Coverage. Enter the annual deductible, which must be at least $3,050 but not more than $4,600. Enter 75% (.75) of the annual deductible on the worksheet. If married filing separately, enter only 37.5% (.375) of the annual deductible on the worksheet. However, if you and your spouse agree to divide the 75% of the annual deductible in a different manner, enter your share on the worksheet.

Line 6

Compensation

Compensation includes wages, salaries, professional fees, and other pay you receive for services you perform. It also includes sales commissions, commissions

Line 5 Limitation Worksheet

Go through this chart for each month of 1999.
See the instructions for line 5.
(Keep for your records)

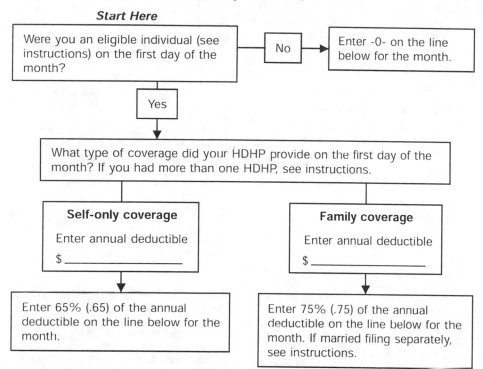

Start Here

Were you an eligible individual (see instructions) on the first day of the month? → No → Enter -0- on the line below for the month.

↓ Yes

What type of coverage did your HDHP provide on the first day of the month? If you had more than one HDHP, see instructions.

Self-only coverage

Enter annual deductible
$ _____

Family coverage

Enter annual deductible
$ _____

Enter 65% (.65) of the annual deductible on the line below for the month.

Enter 75% (.75) of the annual deductible on the line below for the month. If married filing separately, see instructions.

Month in 1999	Amount from chart above
January	_____
February	_____
March	_____
April	_____
May	_____
June	_____
July	_____
August	_____
September	_____
October	_____
November	_____
December	_____
Total for all months	_____

Limitation. Divide the total by 12. Enter here and on line 5 . . . . _____

on insurance premiums, pay based on a percentage of profit, tips, and bonuses. Generally, these amounts are included on the Form(s) W-2 you receive from your employer(s). Compensation also includes net earnings from self-employment, but only for a trade or business in which your personal services are a material income-producing factor. Generally, this amount is shown on the Schedule SE (Form 1040) you complete for your business or farm.

Compensation does not include any amounts received as a pension or annuity and does not include any amount received as deferred compensation.

Line 7

If you (or your employer) contributed more to your MSA than is allowable, you may have to pay a tax on excess contributions. Figure your excess contributions using the instructions below. See **Form 5329**, Additional Taxes Attributable to IRAs, Other Qualified Retirement Plans, Annuities, Modified Endowment Contracts, and MSAs, to figure the additional tax.

Excess Contributions You Make

To figure your excess contributions, subtract your deductible contributions limit (line 7) from your actual contributions (line 4). Do not include rollovers.

However, you can withdraw some or all of your excess contributions for 1999 and they will not be taxed as an excess contribution if:

● You make the withdrawal by the due date, including extensions, of your 1999 tax return,

● You do not claim a deduction for the amount of the withdrawn contribution, and

● You also withdraw any income earned on the withdrawn contributions and include the earnings as "other income" on your tax return for the year you withdraw the contributions and earnings.

Excess Employer Contributions

For each employer, figure the excess employer contributions as the excess, if any, of the employer's contributions over the **smaller** of (a) your limitation on line 5 or (b) your compensation from the employer. If the excess was not included in income on Form W-2, you must report it as "other income" on your tax return.

However, you can withdraw some or all of the excess employer contributions for 1999 and they will not be taxed as an excess contribution if:

● You make the withdrawal by the due date, including extensions, of your 1999 tax return,

● You do not claim an exclusion from income for the amount of the withdrawn contribution, and

- You also withdraw any income earned on the withdrawn contributions and include the earnings as "other income" on your tax return for the year in which you withdraw the contributions and earnings.

Part III—MSA Distributions

Line 8a

Enter the total MSA distributions you and your spouse received in 1999 from all MSAs. These amounts should be shown in box 1 of Form 1099-MSA.

Line 8b

Enter any excess contributions (and the earnings on those excess contributions) included on line 8a that were withdrawn by the due date, including extensions, of your return. See the instructions for line 7 on page 3.

If any distributions you received in 1999 were rolled over, include that amount on line 8b.

Rollovers

A rollover is a tax-free distribution (withdrawal) of assets from one MSA that is reinvested in another. Generally, you must complete the rollover within 60 days following the distribution. See **Pub. 590,** Individual Retirement Arrangements (IRAs), for more details and additional requirements regarding rollovers.

Note: *If you instruct the trustee of your MSA to transfer funds directly to another MSA, the transfer is **not** considered a rollover. **Do not** include the amount transferred in income, deduct it as a contribution, or include it as a distribution on line 8a.*

Line 9

In general, include on line 9 distributions from all MSAs in 1999 that were used for the qualified medical expenses (see page 1) of the account holder and his or her spouse or dependents. However, if a contribution was made to an MSA in 1999 (by you or your employer), do not include on line 9 withdrawals from an MSA if the individual for whom the expenses were incurred was not covered by an HDHP or was covered by a plan that was not an HDHP (other than the exceptions noted on page 1) at the time the expenses were incurred.

Example. In 1999, you were covered by an HDHP with self-only coverage and your spouse was covered by a health plan that was not an HDHP. You made contributions to an MSA for 1999. You cannot include on line 9 withdrawals made from the MSA to pay your spouse's medical expenses incurred in 1999 because your spouse was covered by a plan that was not an HDHP.

 You may not take a deduction on Schedule A (Form 1040) for any amount you include on line 9.

Lines 11a and 11b

Check the box on line 11a if the account holder who received the distribution from an MSA in 1999 met any of the exceptions to the 15% tax. Enter on line 11b 15% (.15) of the portion, if any, of line 10 to which the exception to the 15% tax does not apply.

Exceptions to the 15% Tax

The 15% tax does not apply if the distribution is made after the account holder—

- Dies,
- Becomes disabled (see page 1), or
- Turns age 65.

Example 1. You turned age 66 during the year and had no MSA during the year. Your wife turned age 63 during the year and received a taxable distribution from her MSA. You do NOT check the box on line 11a in this case because your spouse (the account holder) did not meet the age exception.

Example 2. Both you and your spouse received taxable distributions from your MSAs in 1999. You were age 65 at the time you received your distributions and your spouse was age 63 when he or she received the distributions. Check the box on line 11a because you met an exception to the 15% tax. However, the 15% tax still applies to your spouse's distributions.

Example 3. You turned age 65 during the year. You received taxable distributions both before and after you turned age 65. Check the box on line 11a because you met an exception to the 15% tax. However, the 15% tax still applies to the distributions you received before you turned age 65.

Death of Account Holder

If the account holder's surviving spouse is the designated beneficiary, the MSA is treated as if the surviving spouse were the account holder. The surviving spouse completes Form 8853 as though the MSA belonged to him or her.

In all other cases, the account ceases to be an MSA as of the date of death. If you are the beneficiary, complete Form 8853 as follows:

1. Write "Death of MSA account holder" across the top of Form 8853.

2. Write the name(s) shown on your tax return and your SSN in the spaces provided at the top of the form and skip Parts I and II.

3. On line 8a, enter the fair market value of the MSA as of the date of death.

4. On line 9, enter qualified medical expenses incurred by the account holder before the date of death that you paid within 1 year after the date of death.

5. Complete the rest of Part III. The distribution is not subject to the 15% tax.

Report any earnings on the account after the date of death as income on your tax return.

Deemed Distributions From MSAs

The following situations result in deemed distributions from your MSA.

1. You or any of your beneficiaries engaged in any transaction prohibited by section 4975 with respect to any of your MSAs, at any time in 1999. Your account ceases to be an MSA as of January 1, 1999, and you must include the fair market value of all assets in the account as of January 1, 1999, on line 8a.

2. You used any portion of any of your MSAs as security for a loan at any time in 1999. You must include the fair market value of the assets used as security for the loan as income on Form 1040, line 21.

Section B—Medicare+Choice MSA Distributions

Complete Section B if you (or your spouse, if married filing jointly) received distributions from a Medicare+Choice MSA in 1999. If both you and your spouse received distributions, complete a separate Form 8853, Section B, for each spouse. Write "Statement" across the top of each Form 8853, fill in the name and SSN, and complete Section B. Then, add lines 12, 13, 14, and 15b from the two statement Forms 8853 and enter the totals for each line on the controlling Form 8853 (the combined Form 8853 for both spouses). If either spouse checked the box on line 15a of the statement Form 8853, check the box on the controlling Form 8853. Attach the statements and the controlling Form 8853 to your tax return.

Medicare+Choice MSA

A Medicare+Choice MSA is an MSA designated as a Medicare+Choice MSA to be used solely to pay the qualified medical expenses of the account holder. To be eligible for a Medicare+Choice MSA, you must be eligible for Medicare and have a high deductible health plan that meets the Medicare guidelines. Contributions to the account can only be made by Medicare. The contributions and any earnings, while in the account, are not taxable to the account holder. A distribution used exclusively to pay for the qualified medical expenses of the account holder is not taxable. Distributions shown on line 12 that are not used for qualified medical expenses of the account holder are taxable and may also be subject to a penalty.

Death of Account Holder

If the designated beneficiary is the account holder's surviving spouse, the Medicare+Choice MSA is treated as a regular MSA (not a Medicare+Choice MSA) of the surviving spouse for distribution purposes. The surviving spouse must report any distributions after the date of death in Section A, Part III, not in Section B. Include on line 9 qualified medical expenses incurred by the account holder before the date of death and paid by the surviving spouse within 1 year after the date of death.

If the designated beneficiary is not the account holder's surviving spouse, the account ceases to be an MSA as of the date of death. If you are the beneficiary, complete Form 8853 as follows:

1. Write "Death of Medicare+Choice MSA account holder" across the top of Form 8853.

2. Write the name(s) shown on your tax return and your SSN in the spaces provided at the top of the form. Skip Parts I and II.

3. On line 12, enter the fair market value of the Medicare+Choice MSA as of the date of death.

4. On line 13, enter qualified medical expenses incurred by the account holder before the date of death that you paid within 1 year after the date of death.

5. Complete line 14.

The distribution is not subject to the 50% tax. Report any earnings on the account after the date of death as income on your tax return.

Line 12

Enter the total of all your Medicare+Choice MSA distributions received in 1999. These amounts should be shown in box 1 of Form 1099-MSA. This amount should not include any erroneous contributions made by Medicare (or any earnings on the erroneous contributions) or any amounts from a trustee-to-trustee transfer from one MSA to another MSA of the same account holder.

Line 13

Enter the distributions received in 1999 from Medicare+Choice MSA(s) that were used for your qualified medical expenses.

 You may not take a deduction on Schedule A (Form 1040) for any amount you include on line 13.

Lines 15a and 15b—Exceptions to the 50% Tax

Check the box on line 15a if the account holder became disabled (see page 1) or died before the date of any distribution included on line 14. Enter on line 15b 50% (.5) of the distributions on line 14 that do not meet either of these exceptions.

Section C—Long-Term Care (LTC) Insurance Contracts

See **Filing Requirements for Section C** on page 6.

Definitions

Policyholder

The policyholder is the person who owns the proceeds of the LTC insurance contract, life insurance contract, or viatical settlement. The policyholder may be the insured individual. This person is required to report the income, regardless of whether the payment is assigned to a third party or parties. In the case of a group contract, the certificate holder is considered to be the policyholder.

LTC Insurance Contract

In general, amounts paid under a **qualified** LTC insurance contract are excluded from your income. However, if you receive per diem payments (see below), the amount you may exclude is limited.

A contract issued after December 31, 1996, is a qualified LTC insurance contract if it meets the requirements of section 7702B, including the requirement that the insured must be a chronically ill individual (see below). A contract issued before January 1, 1997, generally is treated as a qualified LTC insurance contract if it met state law requirements for LTC insurance contracts and it has not been materially changed.

Per Diem Payments

Per diem payments are payments of a fixed amount made on a periodic basis without regard to actual expenses incurred. Box 3 of Form 1099-LTC should indicate whether the payments were per diem payments.

Chronically Ill Individual

A chronically ill individual is someone who has been certified (at least annually) by a licensed health care practitioner as—

1. Being unable to perform at least two activities of daily living (ADLs) (eating, toileting, transferring, bathing, dressing, and continence), without substantial assistance from another individual, for at least 90 days, due to a loss of functional capacity; or

2. Requiring substantial supervision to protect the individual from threats to health and safety due to severe cognitive impairment.

Accelerated Death Benefits

Generally, amounts paid as accelerated death benefits under a life insurance contract or under certain viatical settlements are fully excludable from your gross income if the insured is a terminally ill individual (see below). Generally,

accelerated death benefits paid with respect to an insured individual who is chronically ill (see above) are excludable from your gross income to the same extent as they would be under a qualified LTC insurance contract.

Line 17

Special rules apply in determining the taxable payments if other individuals received per diem payments under a qualified LTC insurance contract or as accelerated death benefits with respect to the insured listed on line 16a. See **Multiple Payees** on page 7 for details.

Line 18

Terminally Ill Individual

A terminally ill individual is any individual who has been certified by a physician as having an illness or physical condition that can reasonably be expected to result in death within 24 months.

Line 20

If you have more than one LTC period, you must separately calculate the taxable amount of the payments received during each LTC period. To do this, complete lines 20 through 28 on separate sections C for each LTC period. Enter the total on line 28 from each separate Section C on the Form 8853 that you attach to your tax return. See the instructions for line 23 for the LTC period.

Line 21

Enter the total accelerated death benefits you received with respect to the insured listed on line 16a. These amounts should be shown in box 2 of Form 1099-LTC. Only include amounts you received while the insured was a chronically ill individual. **Do not** include amounts you received while the insured was a terminally ill individual. If the insured was redesignated from chronically ill to terminally ill in 1999, only include on line 21 payments received **before** the insured was certified as terminally ill.

Line 23

The number of days in your LTC period depends on which method you choose to define the LTC period. Generally, you may choose either the **Contract Period** method or the **Equal Payment Rate** method. However, special rules apply if other persons also received per diem payments in 1999 under a qualified LTC insurance contract or as accelerated death benefits with respect to the insured listed on line 16a. See **Multiple Payees** on page 7 for details.

Method 1—Contract Period

Under this method your LTC period is the same period as that used by the

Filing Requirements for Section C

Go through this chart for each insured person for whom you received long-term care (LTC) payments.

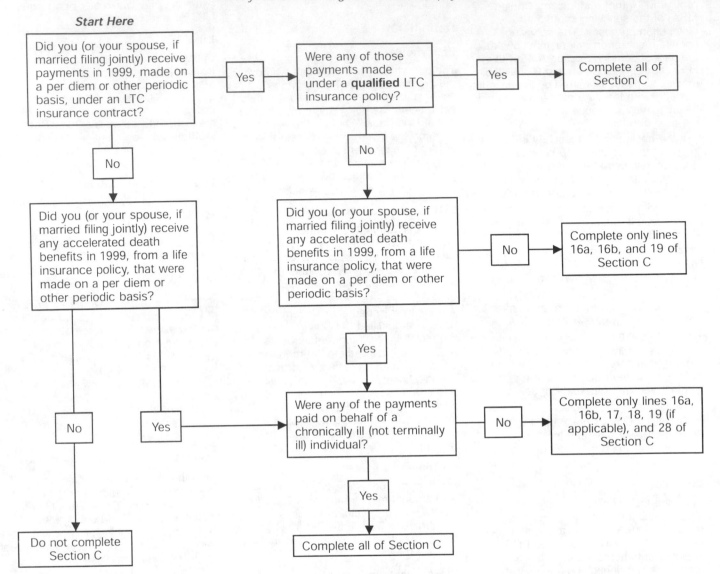

Start Here

Did you (or your spouse, if married filing jointly) receive payments in 1999, made on a per diem or other periodic basis, under an LTC insurance contract? → **Yes** → Were any of those payments made under a **qualified** LTC insurance policy? → **Yes** → Complete all of Section C

→ **No**

Did you (or your spouse, if married filing jointly) receive any accelerated death benefits in 1999, from a life insurance policy, that were made on a per diem or other periodic basis?

→ **No** (under qualified question)

Did you (or your spouse, if married filing jointly) receive any accelerated death benefits in 1999, from a life insurance policy, that were made on a per diem or other periodic basis? → **No** → Complete only lines 16a, 16b, and 19 of Section C

→ **Yes**

Were any of the payments paid on behalf of a chronically ill (not terminally ill) individual? → **No** → Complete only lines 16a, 16b, 17, 18, 19 (if applicable), and 28 of Section C

No → Do not complete Section C

Yes →

→ **Yes** → Complete all of Section C

---

insurance company under the contract to compute the benefits it pays you. For example, if the insurance company computes your benefits on a daily basis, your LTC period is 1 day.

 If you choose this method for defining the LTC period(s) and different LTC insurance contracts for the same insured use different contract periods, then all such LTC contracts must be treated as computing benefits on a daily basis.

Method 2—Equal Payment Rate

Under this method, your LTC period is the period during which the insurance company uses the same payment rate to compute your benefits. For example, you would have two LTC periods if the insurance contract computes payments at a rate of $175 per day from February 1, 1999, through May 31, 1999, and then

at a rate of $195 per day from June 1, 1999, through December 31, 1999. The first LTC period is 120 days (from February 1 through May 31) and the second LTC period is 214 days (from June 1 through December 31).

You may choose this method even if you have more than one qualified LTC insurance contract covering the same period. For example, you have one insurance contract that pays $100 per day from March 1, 1999, through December 31, 1999, and you have a second insurance contract that pays $1,500 per month from March 1, 1999, through December 31, 1999. You have one LTC period because each payment rate does not vary during the LTC period of March 1 through December 31. However, you would have two LTC periods if the facts were the same except that the second insurance contract did not begin making payments until May 1, 1999. The first LTC

period is 61 days (from March 1 through April 30) and the second LTC period is 245 days (from May 1 through December 31).

Line 24

Qualified LTC services are necessary diagnostic, preventive, therapeutic, curing, treating, mitigating, and rehabilitative services, and maintenance or personal care services, required to treat a chronically ill individual (see page 5) under a plan of care prescribed by a licensed health care practitioner.

Line 26

Enter the reimbursements you received or **expect to receive** through insurance or otherwise for qualified LTC services provided for the insured for LTC periods in 1999. Box 3 of Form 1099-LTC should indicate whether the payments were made on a reimbursement basis.

Do not include on line 26 any reimbursements for qualified LTC services you received under a contract issued before August 1, 1996. However, you must include reimbursements if the contract was exchanged or modified after July 31, 1996, to increase per diem payments or reimbursements.

Multiple Payees

If you checked "Yes" on lines 17 and 18 and the **only** payments you received were accelerated death benefits that were paid because the insured was terminally ill, skip lines 19 through 27 and enter zero on line 28.

In all other cases in which you checked "Yes" on line 17, attach a statement duplicating lines 20 through 28 of the form. This attachment should show the **aggregate computation** for **all** persons who received per diem payments under a qualified LTC insurance contract or as accelerated death benefits because the insured was chronically ill. Each person must use the same LTC period. If all the recipients of payments cannot agree on which LTC period to use, the Contract Period method must be used.

After completing the attachment, determine your share of the per diem limitation and any taxable payments. The per diem limitation is allocated first to the insured to the extent of the total payments the insured received. If the insured is married and files a joint return and the insured's spouse is one of the policyholders, the per diem limitation is allocated first to them to the extent of the payments they both received. Any remaining limitation is allocated among the other policyholders pro rata based on the payments they received in 1999.

Enter your share of the per diem limitation and the taxable payments on lines 27 and 28. **Leave lines 23 through 26 blank.**

Example 1

Elsie was chronically ill throughout 1999 and received 12 monthly payments on a per diem basis from a qualified LTC insurance contract. She was paid $2,000 per month ($24,000 total). Elsie incurred expenses for qualified LTC services of $100 per day ($36,500). She was reimbursed for one-half of those expenses ($18,250). Elsie uses the equal payment rate method and therefore has

a single benefit period for 1999 (January 1–December 31). Elsie completes lines 22 through 28 of Form 8853 as follows:

Line	Amount
22	$24,000 ($2,000 x 12 mos.)
23	$69,350 ($190 x 365 days)
24	$36,500 ($100 x 365 days)
25	$69,350
26	$18,250 ($50 x 365 days)
27	$51,100
28	$-0-

Example 2

The facts are the same as in Example 1, except Elsie's son, Sam, and daughter, Deborah, each also own a qualified LTC insurance contract under which Elsie is the insured. Neither Sam nor Deborah incurred any costs for qualified LTC services for Elsie in 1999. From July 1, 1999, through December 31, 1999, Sam received per diem payments of $2,700 per month ($16,200 total) and Deborah received per diem payments of $1,800 per month ($10,800 total). Elsie, Sam, and Deborah agree to use the equal payment rate method to determine their LTC periods.

There are two LTC periods. The first is 181 days (from January 1 through June 30) during which the per diem payments were $2,000 per month. The second is 184 days (from July 1 through December 31) during which the aggregate per diem payments were $6,500 per month ($2,000 under Elsie's contract + $2,700 under Sam's contract + $1,800 under Deborah's contract).

An aggregate statement must be completed for the second LTC period and attached to Elsie, Sam, and Deborah's forms.

Step 1. They complete a statement for Elsie for the first LTC period as follows:

Line	Amount
22	$12,000 ($2,000 x 6 mos.)
23	$34,390 ($190 x 181 days)
24	$18,100 ($100 x 181 days)
25	$34,390
26	$9,050 ($50 x 181 days)
27	$25,340
28	$ -0-

Step 2. They complete the aggregate statement for the second LTC period as follows:

Line	Amount
22	$39,000 ($6,500 x 6 mos.)
23	$34,960 ($190 x 184 days)
24	$18,400 ($100 x 184 days)
25	$34,960
26	$9,200 ($50 x 184 days)
27	$25,760
28	$13,240

Step 3. They allocate the aggregate per diem limitation of $25,760 on line 27 among Elsie, Sam, and Deborah. Because Elsie is the insured, the per diem limitation is allocated first to her to the extent of the per diem payments she received during the second LTC period ($12,000). The remaining per diem limitation of $13,760 is allocated between Sam and Deborah.

Allocation ratio to Sam: Sam receives 60% of the remaining limitation because the $16,200 he received during the second LTC period is 60% of the $27,000 received by both Sam and Deborah during the second LTC period.

Allocation ratio to Deborah: Deborah receives 40% of the remaining limitation because the $10,800 she received during the second LTC period is 40% of the $27,000 received by both Sam and Deborah during the second LTC period.

Step 4. Elsie, Sam, and Deborah each complete Form 8853 as follows.

Elsie's Form 8853:

Line	1st LTC Period	2nd LTC Period	Form 8853
22	$12,000	$12,000	$24,000
27	$25,340	$12,000	$37,340
28	$ 0	$ 0	$ 0

Sam's Form 8853:

Line	1st LTC Period	2nd LTC Period	Form 8853
22	$ 0	$16,200	$16,200
27	$ 0	$8,256	$8,256
28	$ 0	$7,944	$7,944

Deborah's Form 8853:

Line	1st LTC Period	2nd LTC Period	Form 8853
22	$ 0	$10,800	$10,800
27	$ 0	$5,504	$5,504
28	$ 0	$5,296	$5,296

Paperwork Reduction Act Notice. We ask for the information on this form to carry out the Internal Revenue laws of the United States. You are required to give us the information. We need it to ensure that you are complying with these laws and to allow us to figure and collect the right amount of tax.

You are not required to provide the information requested on a form that is subject to the Paperwork Reduction Act unless the form displays a valid OMB control number. Books or records relating to a form or its instructions must be retained as long as their contents may become material in the administration of any Internal Revenue law. Generally, tax returns and return information are confidential, as required by section 6103.

The time needed to complete and file this form will vary depending on individual circumstances. The estimated average time is:

Recordkeeping.................. 1 hr., 19 min.

Learning about the law
or the form .... 34 min.

Preparing the form .... 1 hr., 30 min.

Copying, assembling,
and sending the form to
the IRS .... 20 min.

If you have comments concerning the accuracy of these time estimates or suggestions for making this form simpler, we would be happy to hear from you. You can write to the Tax Forms Committee, Western Area Distribution Center, Rancho Cordova, CA 95743-0001. **DO NOT** send the form to this address. Instead, see **Where Do You File?** in the Form 1040 instructions.